Presented to:

____

By:

____

Date: __________________

I welcome and seek your ideas, but do not bring me small ideas; bring me big ideas to match our future. – Arnold Schwarzenegger

Whatever universe a professor believes in must at any rate be a universe that lends itself to lengthy discourse. A universe definable in two sentences is something for which the professorial intellect has no use. No faith in anything of that cheap kind!
– William James

Good company and good discourse are the very sinews of virtue. – Izaak Walton

To strive, to seek, to find,
and not to yield. – Alfred Lord Tennyson

The apple cannot be stuck back on the tree of Knowledge; once we begin to see, we are doomed and challenged to seek the strength to see more, not less. – Arthur Miller

A good discourse is that from which nothing can be retrenched without cutting into the quick. – Saint Francis de Sales

That's what we're missing. We're missing argument. We're missing debate. We're missing colloquy. We're missing all sorts of things. Instead, we're accepting.
– Studs Terkel

Let your discourse with men of business be short and comprehensive.
– George Washington

A BROTHER ASKS

Volume 1

Uncommon Discourses about Hiram

John S. Nagy

A Brother Asks – Volume 1
Uncommon Discourses about Hiram

Also Author of:

- The Craft Unmasked – *The Uncommon Origin of Freemasonry and Its Practice*
- The Journeyman Papers
- Building Hiram
- Building Boaz
- Building Athens
- Building Janus
- Building Perpends
- Building Ruffish
- Building Cement
- Building Free Men
- Provoking Success
- Emotional Awareness Made Easy

Publisher: Promethean Genesis Publishing
PO Box 636, Lutz FL 33548-0636

ISBN-13: 978-0-9911094-4-9

Second Printing, March 2018
Published in the United States of America
Book Editing, Design and Illustration
by John S. Nagy

Books available through www.coach.net
Cover Graphic: La Mort d'Hiram;
Le Soleil Mystique 1853

Dedication

To my Brother Builders Nick, Jeff, Dale, R.J., Coleman, Jason, Albert, Kevin, Nicholas, and Luther: *I offer a sincere and heartfelt thank you for helping me reveal this book.*

To all my Brothers who want what is discussed in this book: *may you find Brothers with whom you may joyfully have such discourse.*

To my future Brother Builders: *may this book help Light your way as you continue your Journey East, Masterfully Building.*

To my two sons: *I look forward to the day you Rise in Mastery so that I may gift this book to you as Masterful Men and Widow's Sons.*

To my lovingly supportive wife
and best friend: when you say,
"Speak from your heart!" you shall
hear it sing *in three part harmony.*

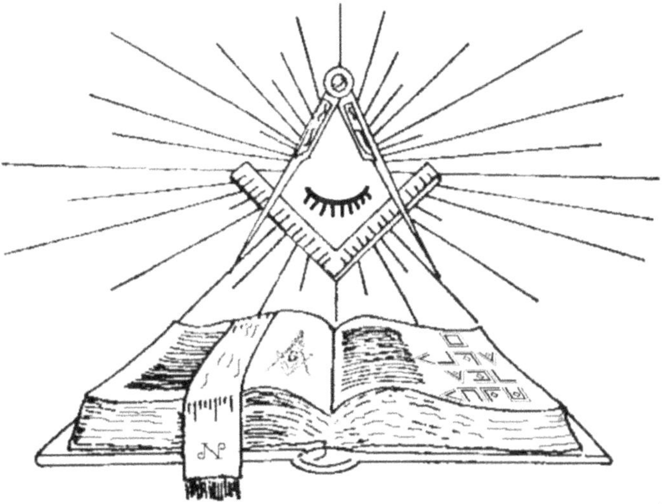

"The Mason who reads, however little, be it only the pages of the monthly magazine to which he subscribes, will entertain higher views of the Institution and enjoy new delights in the possession of these views. Such a Mason must be an indifferent one. He has laid no foundation for zeal.

If this indifference, instead of being checked, becomes more widely spread, the result is too apparent. Freemasonry must step down from the elevated position which she has been struggling, through the efforts of her scholars, to maintain, and our lodges, instead of becoming resorts for speculative and philosophical thought, will deteriorate into social clubs or mere benefit societies.

With so many rivals in that field, her struggle for a prosperous life will be a hard one.

The ultimate success of Masonry depends on the intelligence of her disciples."

(Excerpt from "Reading Masons & Masons Who Do Not Read" – Brother Albert Mackey, 1874; author of "The Encyclopedia of Freemasonry and Its Kindred Sciences...")

Suitable & Fair Warnings

This document contains a series of critical *Master Mason level* connections that might at first cause emotions of extreme discomfort, disgust, irritation, shock, and dismay, especially if you are a member of the Society of Free & Accepted Masons. It is highly recommended that you read through the entire book before you draw any rash, superficial and wholly unsupported conclusions. *Your efforts shall be rewarded!*

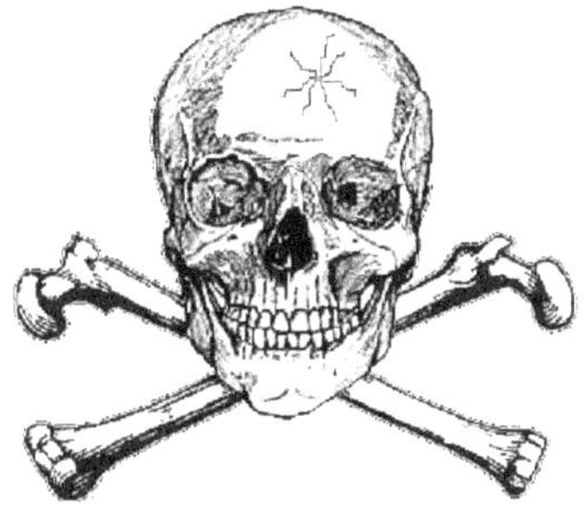

When it comes to Freemasonic ritual, it is always best not to discuss anything therein contained with anyone who has yet to experience it legitimately, fully, and completely. In this light, it is highly recommended that you not discuss in depth anything within this book with anyone *who is not a Master Mason and who has yet to read or hear it thoroughly & completely for himself.* Doing so, shallowly revealing anything in this book to others who have yet to read it through or hear it thoroughly, will both ruin the intended experience of the book for them and prevent you from having a rich discussion about it with an informed person.

As of the first publishing of this book, no Grand Lodge exists that publically or privately shares this author's view of what is herein contained.

Preface

One very frustrating threefold experience that all initiates have in common is knowing something exists, knowing that it is hidden in plain sight and not knowing how they must change to see it for themselves.

Discourse between Brothers and Fellows can bring about some delightfully challenging exchanges and awesomely entertaining insights into what ritual communicates and about how members experience and understand it. I've had a lot of these colloquies exchanged over the years. Each has brought to light deeper and fuller understandings into the third degree allegory and how it can be applied toward living a fuller and more masterful life.

Many of these conversations occurred in text form exchanged in forums, private messenger systems and texts. Many became standard *"go to"* references used when a topic or subject was being revisited by either the same parties or new colloquists to the discussion. Ultimately, these dialogs were refined and cataloged for future reference, knowing full well that present conversations would be rehashed and revised repeatedly.

In time, the value of these reference files increased tremendously with every addition and modification. I found some of the questions being asked so often that I posted some of them on my blog and gleefully shared a link to it when the subject came up once again.

Eventually I amassed more than two books filled with these exchanges. I soon began the process of consolidating them so that the information would flow smoothly and without any deep cowans[i] that would cause problems when each was offered.

This is the first of two books that have been put together as brotherly discourses. The second one will follow after it has been further refined.

This writing effort covers the third degree drama and focuses heavily upon its allegorical and symbolic aspects. It delves into historical background and is overflowing with connections and supportive information that many Brothers have not yet even begun to imagine.

Obviously, there are things within the third degree that cannot and should not be written. As you engage in what it has to offer you, please keep in mind the spirit in which they were originally exchanged. These are a direct result of Brothers seeking Light.

It is hoped the manner in which this information is presented herein will assist you, and all those who are touched by it, to better grasp the lessons and insights the third degree allegory has to offer.

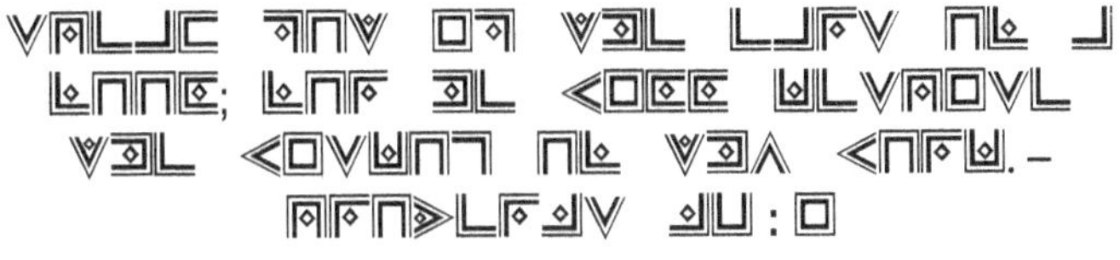

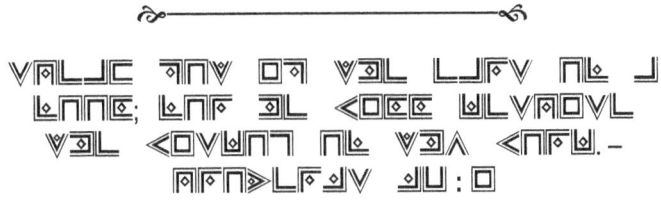

[i] hollows, indents, crevices, holes, etc

Definitions

Colloquy (n.) plural *colloquies*

1. (*Formal*) a discourse, conversation or dialog; a conversational exchange; conference.
2. (*Christianity*) a church court held by certain Reformed denominations.
3. (*Law*) a discussion during a trial in which a judge ensures that defendants understand what is taking place in the trial and what their rights are.
4. A gathering for discussion of philosophical or theological questions; an informal conference on philosophical, religious or theological matters.
5. A literary work in dialogue form; a written discourse.

[*Origin*] mid-15c., *"discourse"*, from Latin *colloquium "conference, conversation,"* literally *"a speaking together,"* from *com- "together"* (see com-) + *-loquium "speaking"*, from *loqui "to speak"* (from PIE root **tolkw- "to speak"*). Meaning *"conversation"* is attested in English from 1580s.

Colloquist (n.) plural *colloquists*

1. One who takes part in colloquy.
2. A colloquy participant.

Dare Enter ye Gates, and
Explore ye Whole Scheme,
True Light there Awaits,
or so It may Seem.

Pass up ye Good Work,
Do Less than one Needs,
Find no More than Fewer
of Mastery's Dreams.

When Words be not Words,
and Names be not Names,
We Lessen Our Folly,
and Strengthen Our Games,

Mysteries We'll Solve,
and Puzzle ye Mages,
Change Lead into Gold,
and Fools into Sages.

Table of Contents

Preface....................iv
Table of Contents....................viii
Introduction....................9
1. Of What to Be Aware....................12
2. Allegory....................15
3. Hiram's Name....................22
4. The Widow's Son....................28
5. The Widowed....................34
6. Denying Hiram....................39
7. The Secrets....................42
8. Rejecting Joppa....................49
9. Ethiopia....................54
10. Wayfaring....................60
11. The Fifteen Ruffians....................62
12. Spotting Craft Ruffians....................69
13. Symbolic Penalties....................71
14. Cowan & Ruffian Insights....................76
15. Ruffian Symbolism....................83
16. Ruffian Meaning....................92
17. Raising Lessons....................107
18. The Grasp....................118
19. Resurrecting Hiram....................123
20. The Substitute....................129
21. The Master's Word....................138
22. Where the Masters Are....................145
23. What Was Lost....................151
24. Substituting the Substitute....................156
Endnotes....................163

Introduction

We approach the kingdom gates when
we realize that words are not words
and names are not names.

The third degree drama has left many a brother scratching his head in confusion as to what it means and how to apply what it reveals toward living more empowering lives. The sheer conciseness of the dialog and the plethora of allusions could take a lifetime to understand, much less apply. Although there have been many books written on the subject, the mass of these texts do not have a frank and open discussion as to its relevance and impact upon men's lives. This had to change.

You are about to experience, through this writing, a multitude of blunt and pointed conversations held between my Brothers and me that have been strung together in bit sized pieces for your fun and pleasure. Each of them occurred over the last fifteen years and in many differing formats from writing to oral discourse.

They continue to reoccur as a result of new Brothers being brought to Light and who have similar questions and observations to share.

These conversations focus upon concepts and insights into manhood and mastery hidden in plain sight within the third degree drama. Each offers tremendous insights into cultivating mastery and dealing with those who refuse to do the same. They are each a wellspring from which to learn and teach others to do likewise.

I believed it was important to take time to immortalize them in book form and to share it with those who could benefit from its reading. I also believe it is important that future generations be able to learn from such conversations so that they too can be teachers to the generations to come.

The intents of presenting them here to you are many fold. By reading and perpending this material, you'll have the opportunity to learn about concepts masked by allegory. You'll also have an opportunity to glean insights into human nature and how human nature runs into gnarly obstacles that cannot be overcome by brute force. You'll hopefully see more of what is hidden in plain sight as a result of how the conversations are designed.

The entirety of this book can be used for self educational purposes. However, I recommend the book be read with other Brothers so that you can discuss the concepts even further than what the book offers. Each section is a conversation starter and should be used as grist for the mill of discourse between Brothers and Fellows.

I offer two closing suggestions. First, read these discourses as if you are listening to two or more Brothers interact. Secondly, it would take very little time and effort to have two or more Brothers act out any one of these colloquies within an open lodge. Imagine acted out these discussions amongst the brethren in ritual fashion and offering the entire lodge and its visitors an opportunity to be educated and entertained. Imagine as well an opportunity to continue these conversations long after each presentation ends.

With this being said, please consider different ways of sharing these dialogs with Brothers. They deserve to get something significant by their attendance in open lodge and there are two dozen conversation starters found herein, two for every month of the year, that you can use within your lodge for all of your lodge and visiting Brothers' benefit.

I hope you find each of them nurturing to your mind, heart and spirit.

Enjoy!

John S. Nagy

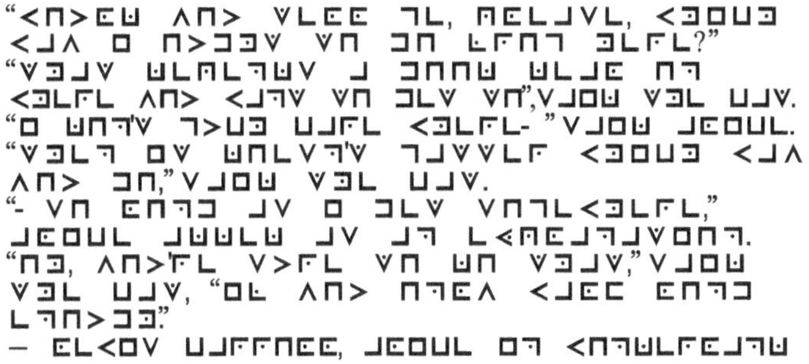

1. Of What to Be Aware

It is the glory of God to conceal a matter, But the glory of kings is to search out a matter.
– Proverbs 25:2

A Brother Asks: Do you have any suggestions as to what I should be aware of while perpending the Third Degree Legend?

Coach: Yes. Just like all Allegory, it reflects two levels of communicated understanding to Candidates.

Brother: Two levels? What do you mean by that?

Coach: There are two specific levels of communication going on at the same time during these Allegorical plays.

Brother: What are these levels?

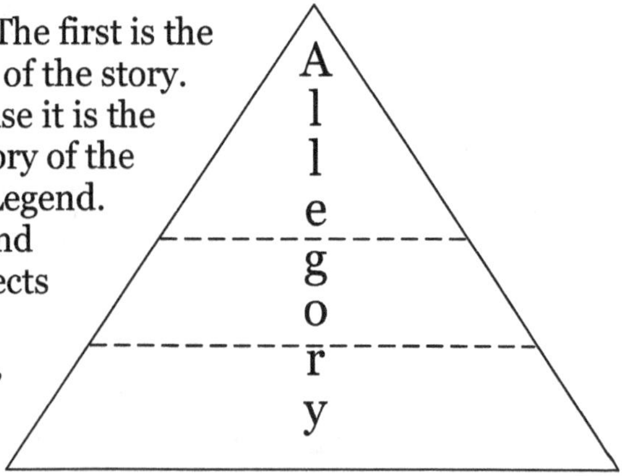

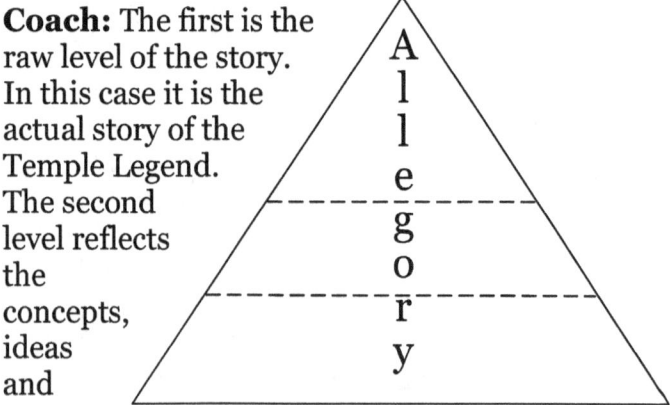

Coach: The first is the raw level of the story. In this case it is the actual story of the Temple Legend. The second level reflects the concepts, ideas and philosophies alluded to within the level one tale.

Brother: Why is this so important?

Coach: Because when you confuse the two you will take things out of context and come to some extremely erroneous conclusions.

Brother: What are some of the erroneous conclusions that you have heard or read?

Coach: That 1) Hiram was resurrected, 2) the story was actual history, 3) the three ruffians and the three grand masters represent actual people. These are all erroneous and wholly unsupported conclusions.

Brother: How do we know this?

Coach: Because close and careful scrutiny of them reveals each to be so.

Brother: Is there something else that needs to be understood?

Coach: Yes. That there is actually a third level that is not often recognized, much less understood.

Brother: What is that?

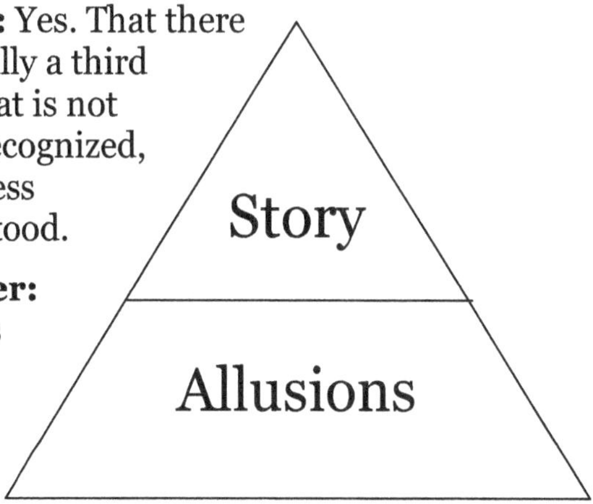

Coach: It is the candidate level.

Brother: The candidate level?

Coach: Yes. These two levels are interwoven within a much bigger story. The candidate comes into this experience with a level of understanding that he is going through a ritual. The drama he experiences is a story within a story that is ritual.

Brother: So, he comes into these ritual experiences believing he is going through a ritual, which is level one.

Coach: Yes

Brother: He is also experiencing ritual when he is put through the drama, which is level two.

Coach: Agreed!

Brother: And finally he comes to find that the drama is actually an allegory, that has a whole different level of meaning beyond the actual ritual and story, which is level three?

Coach: Yes.

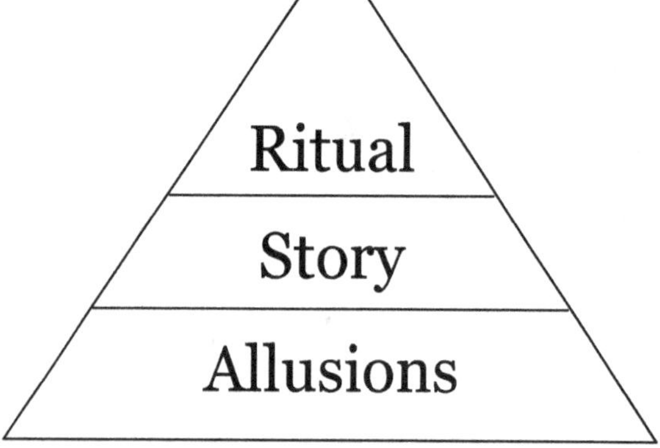

2. Allegory

Call to Me and I will answer you, and I will tell you great and mighty things, which you do not know. – Jeremiah 33:3

A Brother Asks: What do members mean when they say the third degree drama is an allegory?

Coach: That's because it is. But in truth, it is a *"morality[1]"*, which is a sub class of allegorical play.

Brother: A morality. Upon which moral does it focus?

Coach: Not a morality in the sense of a moral. It is a morality in the sense of a morality play.

Brother: A morality play?

Coach: Yes!

Brother: What's that?

Coach: A morality is a type of allegorical drama with personified abstract qualities as the main characters that present lessons about good conduct and character.

Brother: Abstract qualities? Can you provide some examples please?

Coach: Yes. Abstract qualities like virtue, vice, good, evil, life, death, youth, age, wisdom, beauty, strength, charity, mercy, temperance, justice, truth, and others. Each is portrayed by actors.

Brother: Interesting. I'm not familiar with them. When were these moralities popular?

Coach: They grew out of the mysteries during the fourteenth century and were popular in the fifteenth and early sixteenth centuries.

Brother: The mysteries? You mean like things that are or were mysterious?

Coach: No. But there are many members within the organization that'll go to their deaths believing that.

Brother: Believing what?

Coach: That the mysteries are things that were hidden, esoteric and mysterious.

Brother: What should they understand?

Coach: That the mysteries within this context referred to the plays that were put on by medieval occupational guilds[2].

Brother: How did the word *"mysteries"* come to define them?

Coach: At the time, *"mystery"* had the same meaning as *"mastery"*, as in, *the "occupation or livelihood"* a man engaged in as a profession.

Brother: Okay. How did they get associated with plays?

Coach: The guilds of the time put on plays in the streets during special and specific times of the year. When they did, local citizens would be entertained and educated by them. The benefit to the guild would be product and service placement, thus allowing them to market their professional offerings and wares.

Brother: The guild members acted?

Coach: Yes, in a quasi-professional way. Their plays were usually short and their serious themes were often tempered by elements of farce.

Brother: Farce?

Coach: Yes! Dramatic plays that used highly improbable situations, stereotyped characters, extravagant exaggerations, & violent horseplay.

Brother: Wait a minute! Some of these elements can be found within the third degree drama!

Coach: Really? Can you provide examples of these?

Brother: Sure! The easiest are the stereotypical characters.

Coach: Such as?

Brother: Ruffians[3] for one. But I would include the Fellow Crafts, the three grand masters, boat captains, and the wayfaring man. They are each stereotypical.

Coach: What else?

Brother: Well, there's the violent horseplay disguised as part of the plot.

Coach: What else?

Brother: There's also the improbable.

Coach: Improbable?

Brother: Yes. Where were the guards?

Coach: Guards? For what would guards be used?

Brother: Hiram Abiff. He was an important and key component in building the temple. Why didn't King Solomon make sure that Hiram was well-guarded?

Coach: Allegory.

Brother: Allegory?

Coach: Precisely! The challenge of allegory, even when it contains elements of farce, is that what you would assume to be part of a believable story is not necessarily reflected within the tale.

Brother: For instance?

Coach: Hiram Abiff was an allegorical character representing *something else*, not someone. Hence what you are actually picking up upon is that Beauty was not protected. It's allegorical and you are correct in your observation!

Brother: Thanks!

Coach: What else?

Brother: There are the improbable situations and extravagant exaggerations?

Coach: Like?

Brother: There are the indiscriminate tool use, the odd and deadly penalties, and the inability to provide a simple word to name three.

Coach: Any other clues?

Brother: Yes. Realistically, the ruffians hiding in the clefts of the rocks could have ambushed the Fellow Crafts seeking them quite easily. In reality, truth and justice shall take you just so far when dealing with real life experienced ruffians.

Coach: What are you saying then?

Brother: There's more going on behind the scenes in this offered allegory than I first gleaned.

Coach: Meaning?

Brother: The play must be studied thoroughly to understand the nuances of all that is being conveyed.

Coach: It certainly should.

Brother: So, that's why allegory is used within ritual!

Coach: Yes. It is used because *it is the Primary Method used throughout history to convey Theological and Philosophical Principles and Concepts*. Such training is invaluable in laying a foundation for future studies of Ancient and Modern Theological & Philosophical Literature.

Brother: Is this why we must train to understand it?

Coach: Very much so. Training to understand allegories is the primary challenge faced by anyone making effort to decode conveyed things that are purposefully masked, veiled, concealed, and/or hidden. This especially applies to things encoded in languages and symbols long forgotten. Keep in mind that its use has some interesting side benefits & annoying side effects.

Brother: What are those side benefits?

Coach: Using allegory provides extremely effective methods of cleverly masking, secretly veiling, carefully concealing, and blatantly hiding valuable information in plain sight.

Brother: What is its annoying side effect?

Coach: Unskilled and ignorant individuals usually make more of allegories than they were ever meant to convey and use them as excuses to do all sorts of insane things.

Brother: Such as?

Coach: They use them to create cultures willing to expend inordinate amounts of time, energy, and other resources toward supporting societies with fictitious histories. They research and act as if their mythic historical accounts actually occurred. They create causes designed to rally their members toward further support.

Brother: What else?

Coach: They use others to build expensive edifices designed to further support these fabrications, research efforts and causes.

Brother: Have you any more to add to this?

Coach: They support and encourage further creations of fictitious historically veiled accounts of their imaginary exploits for posterity.

Brother: What makes allegory fun?

Coach: Did you not hear my last Response?

Brother: Okay. Let me ask a different way. What makes allegory interesting?

Coach: It invites curious minds to embrace contrasting and conflicting information and to dig deeper to cultivate insights into things, people, issues, and situations that require them to transcend what might appear contradictory at first.

Brother: So, in many ways it is a training ground where, by your participation, you are exposed to such things in the hope that you shall use the experience and materials to stimulate further personal development?

Coach: Exactly!

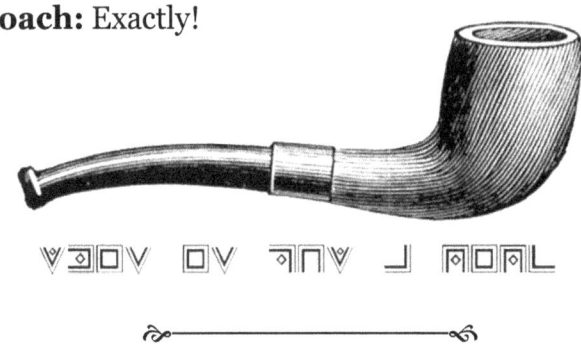

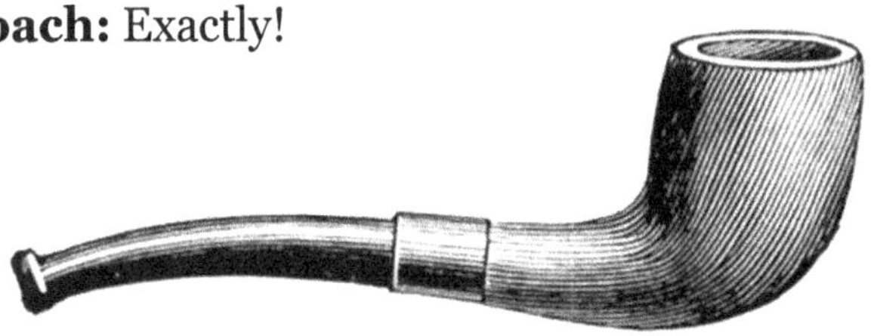

V⊐□V □V ⅂∩V ⅃ ⊓□⊓L

ᑎ□ᑌV>ᒥLV ᒧᒥL ᒣᑎV V⊐L V⊐□ᒣ⊐V V⊐L∧ ᒥLᑎᒥLVLᒣV, ᒣL□V⊐Lᒥ ᒧᒥL <ᑎᒥᑌV <⊐ᒧV V⊐L∧ ᑌLᒣᑎVL. V⊐L <ᑎᒥᑌ ᑌLᒣᑎV□ᒣ⊐ V⊐L ᒣᒧVVLᒥ'V <ᑎᒥᑌ □V ᒣᑎV <⊐ᒧV □V ᑌLᒣᑎVLV, ⊐LᒣᑌL □V ᑌᒧᒣᒣᑎV ᑌᑎ <⊐ᒧV V⊐L ᒣᒧVVLᒥ'V <ᑎᒥᑌ ᑌᒧᒣ ᑌᑎ.

3. Hiram's Name

The people were surprised when they heard him. "How does he know so much when he hasn't been trained?" they asked. — John 7:15

A Brother Asks: What is alluded to by Hiram Abiff's name?

Coach: There's a lot.

Brother: Good! I was hoping there was. Where would you recommend we begin?

Coach: I recommend looking up each name's meaning.

Brother: I have.

Coach: What did you find?

Brother: The name *"Hiram"* means, *"my brother is exalted."*

Coach: Did you look up *"exalted?"*

Brother: Yes, I did. It means, *"elevated or raised."*

Coach: What do you get when you put the two meanings together?

Brother: When I put it together it means, *"my brother is raised."*

Coach: What do you think about this?

Brother: It's interesting that the name of the character the candidate is playing means exactly what will occur for the candidate when the story comes to closure.

Coach: Do you think that this is coincidental?

Brother: No. I think it is deliberate and contrived.

Coach: Why?

Brother: Because the story is deliberately designed for the candidate's benefit and it is making every effort to communicate this using several layers of meaning.

Coach: Yes it is. What does the name's meaning say to you?

Brother: That by playing the role of Hiram, I am a Brother who is raised.

Coach: I concur. What did you find when you looked up the word, *"Abiff."*

Brother: I get a lot of conflicting information.

Coach: Like what?

Brother: For instance, from one source I get that it means, *"my father."* That doesn't make any sense.

Coach: Are you familiar with the use of titles?

Brother: Yes. Are you telling me indirectly that *"my father"* is a title?

Coach: Yes. I am doing just that.

Brother: But what would such a title mean?

Coach: It could mean a lot of things. However, in this case, it means something very specific.

Brother: What's that?

Coach: It means, *"someone's teacher"* and alludes more specifically to, "someone's *spiritual* teacher."

Brother: So *"Abiff"* means *"a spiritual teacher?"*

Coach: No. It means, "*someone's* spiritual teacher."

Brother: Why do you emphasize *"someone"* in this?

Coach: Because the teaching is deliberately associated with a specific human being, and not just anyone.

Brother: So, Hiram was someone's spiritual teacher?

Coach: He certainly was, according to his title.

Brother: Yes. It would be a title. I can see this now.

Coach: What happens when you put the two meanings together?

Brother: For the name, *"Hiram Abiff?"*

Coach: Yes.

Brother: I get, *"My Brother is Raised and he is Someone's Spiritual Teacher."*

Coach: Yes. That's a powerful meaning. Wouldn't you agree?

Brother: I do agree.

Coach: So, who do you think his first student was?

Brother: Hiram's first student?

Coach: Yes. And as it related specifically to the candidate?

Brother: The candidate?

Coach: Yes, if the candidate is playing the role of Hiram Abiff, then we are really asking *"who was the candidate's first student?"*

Brother: That's an interesting twist. But it makes sense.

Coach: Good. So, who would it be?

Brother: Well, it would have to be himself.

Coach: Why's that?

Brother: Because, if the candidate did the Work alluded to by the first two degrees, he would have *prepared to learn* and then *learned how to learn*.

Coach: Which means what?

Brother: He taught himself how to learn.

Coach: Yes. But why was the word *"spiritual"* added to the meaning?

Brother: That has to do with the Work he was supposed to do in the previous two degrees, no?

Coach: It has everything to do with the previous degree Work.

Brother: How so?

Coach: When you do the Apprentice Work, you are symbolically greeted in the next degree by having a point raised above the square.

Brother: What does this mean?

Coach: It means that you have completed the Work and subjugated your physical being to your spiritual being.

Brother: Where are you getting this?

Coach: From the Square and Compasses. The Square represents the physical. The Compasses represents the spiritual.

Brother: So, when the spiritual aspect of the candidate rises above the physical, this is pointed out by the configuration of the Square and Compasses?

Coach: Yes.

Brother: And when both points are elevated above the square, it is an indication that the candidate has raised themselves spiritually?

Coach: That's my take on it.

Brother: So that effort, the Work the candidate does to raise himself to a spiritual level, earns him the two fold title, *"Hiram Abiff?"*

Coach: Why did you say two-fold title?

Brother: Because it's clear that it is not a name.

Coach: How do you reason this?

Brother: Because the very meanings assigned to each are directly attributed to the Work that the candidate is supposed to do to earn the meanings assigned.

Coach: Agreed! So, what are you getting from this exchange?

Brother: A lot!

Coach: The lesson Brother. What's the lesson?

Brother: Oh! Yes. The lesson...

Coach: Yes!

Brother: Well, for one, Hiram Abiff is not a name. It's an earned title that describes what he has become as a result of doing the Work one must do to become Masterful.

Coach: Yes. And?

Brother: To exemplify Hiram Abiff, you must do the same?

Coach: Which is?

Brother: Raise yourself by learning how to learn well enough to teach yourself and then others.

Coach: I concur!

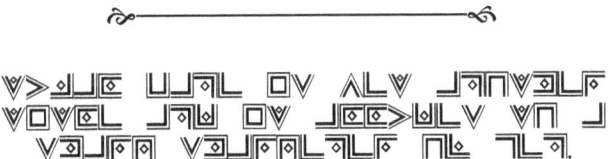

4. The Widow's Son

"I am about to go the way of all the earth,"
he said. "So be strong, act like a man,
— 1 Kings 2:2

A Brother Asks: Who was the King referring to when he was asking for help for *"The Widow's Son?"*

Coach: That's an awesome question!

Brother: Why do you say that?

Coach: Because it shows you have some doubt as to which widow's son he was referring.

Brother: Of course I have doubt.

Coach: But why?

Brother: Because Hiram Abiff was dead when the comment was made.

Coach: And?

Brother: Prior to Hiram's death, he was not the only widow's son within the Morality[4].

Coach: Are you saying there was more than one widow's son present?

Brother: Yes, I am. There was more than one!

Coach: Who else were widow's sons?

Brother: King Solomon and King Hiram were both widows' sons at the moment of the allegorical reenactment.

Coach: Yes. I agree. And you would like to know if King Solomon was referring to dead Hiram, live Hiram or himself?

Brother: Yes! I do!

Coach: Could he be referring to King Hiram?

Brother: How is that?

Coach: King Hiram was having a very difficult time raising dead Hiram's body out of the grave. So maybe it was King Hiram that King Solomon was referring to.

Brother: It could have been. But wasn't King Solomon a widow's son too!

Coach: Yes, he was. So, was King Solomon referring to himself because he was not getting the results he wanted from King Hiram?

Brother: It could be this possibility too.

Coach: Could there be a fourth possibility?

Brother: I had not thought about that.

Coach: When you do, to whom do you think it could also refer?

Brother: It could refer to the candidate.

Coach: Yes. It could.

Brother: And moreover, when I think about it further, I believe at the allegorical level, it *has* to be the candidate.

Coach: I agree! What compels you toward this conclusion?

Brother: The whole degree is for the candidate's benefit.

Coach: And?

Brother: It would not make sense to have anything within the ritual performance that was not for the benefit of the candidate.

Coach: Agreed. Why do you think they were each a widow's son?

Brother: Scriptures indicate that King Solomon's Father, King David, was dead by the time of the temple being built.

Coach: Agreed! What about King Hiram?

Brother: He too was a Widow's son at the time of the Temple being built.

Coach: Agreed! And that is what makes you believe they were widows' sons?

Brother: Yes.

Coach: Could there be another reason?

Brother: By the manner in which you ask, can I take it that there's another reason?

Coach: Certainly you can!

Brother: Does it have to do with an allegorical lesson?

Coach: Yes! Would you like to walk through it with me?

Brother: Of course!

Coach: Great! We both agree that a man who no longer has a biological father in his life is a widow's son.

Brother: Yes.

Coach: Being a man without a biological father, and barring his being adopted or answering to another, would that mean he would be his own man?

Brother: Certainly!

Coach: Can you take it from here?

Brother: Let me try.

Coach: Okay.

Brother: You are alluding to a condition.

Coach: Yes I am.

Brother: And that condition exists whenever and wherever a man finds himself without a physical father figure of any sort.

Coach: Yes. I am.

Brother: And whenever and wherever that condition exists for a man, he could metaphorically be referred to as *"a widow's son"* by virtue of being fatherless.

Coach: Agreed!

Brother: If I put this all together, the moment you become your own man, no longer being fathered or answering to a father figure, either by choice or by chance, you have become a widow's son.

Coach: Why is that?

Brother: Because for all intents and purposes, your father is dead and all who would father you are dead.

Coach: And what are the ramifications, my Brother?

Brother: Well, for one, you could not call other men *"father."*

Coach: And what would you call them instead, especially if they were family?

Brother: I could call them *"Brother."*

Coach: Yes, you could.

Brother: So, if I am a widow's son, I would treat other men as my equals when they too have this condition in their lives. This would include my sons when each of them became his own man!

Coach: How so?

Brother: Because by each of them being his own man, they would not look to me or any other man to be their father.

Coach: Are you saying that for a man to become a widow's son, he must first become his own man?

Brother: I guess I am.

Coach: You guess?

Brother: No! I know this to be true, and I stand by it!

Coach: Okay. It sounded like you were unsure; hence, my question.

Brother: Thank you, my Brother.

Coach: You are most welcome!

Brother: Is that it?

Coach: Not if you want to explore the lesson.

Brother: I do!

Coach: So, what is it?

Brother: *"The Widow's Son"* is not a reference *to a person.*

Coach: What is it?

Brother: It's an *earned title!*

Coach: Denoting?

Brother: A person who has earned the right to be his own man, answering to none other.

5. The Widowed

"Therefore, come out from their midst and be separate," says the Lord. "and do not touch what is unclean; and I will welcome you.
— 2 Corinthians 6:17

A Brother Asks: Okay, I know who the widow's son is, but who's the widow?

Coach: Like so many other things that are presented to us in Allegorical form, it, *"The Widow"* to whom the son is connected, is not a *"who"*; it is a *"what."*

Brother: A what?

Coach: Yes, a what! When you know to what it is that the *"Widow"* is referring, it also tells you what you need to focus upon to become its offspring.

Brother: So, to what is the Widow referring?

Coach: Should you want to pursue this in depth, I recommend you look at the intimate connection between the words *"winnow"* and *"widow."*

Brother: Okay. I see that the two hold *"separation"* in common.

Coach: Yes, they do. Both allude to what you must do to become the offspring of specific actions that you must take to earn the title, *"The Widow's Son."*

Brother: What must a person do to become this offspring?

Coach: Great Question! Ask yourself, what widowing are you required to do through your Masonic journey from profane to mastery and in what must you actively participate to achieve that mastery?

Brother: Okay. I get it. Widowing means separating.

Coach: Yes!

Brother: By the very act of joining and going through the first degree, I separate myself from the profane of the world.

Coach: Yes, you do!

Brother: I imagine that there's more to it.

Coach: Yes. What Apprentice Work does ritual direct you to do?

Brother: Divest myself of vices and superfluities.

Coach: What does divestment entail?

Brother: Knowing from what to separate, and then separating from it. When I divest myself from vices and superfluities, I separate myself from them.

Coach: Yes. And if you do all the Work that is pointed out by the degree, who else do you separate yourself from?

Brother: The weak and unnecessarily burdened.

Coach: How so?

Brother: The first degree Work is designed to strengthen and unburden those who do it. Those who do not do it remain weak and unnecessarily burdened.

Coach: So, by doing the Work of this degree, you separated yourself from both those who are weak and burdened and also from weakness and unnecessary burdens?

Brother: Yes. I'm beginning to see a pattern here.

Coach: Good. What does completing the apprentice Work do for you?

Brother: It brings order to the chaos of my heart and brings me to maturity!

Coach: It certainly should!

Brother: Let me take a shot at the second degree Work.

Coach: Sure. What have you got so far?

Brother: By doing the Fellow Craft Work.

Coach: Which is?

Brother: Climbing those stairs!

Coach: What stairs?

Brother: The seven liberal arts and sciences.

Coach: Meaning?

Brother: Studying and ingraining them into my very being.

Coach: What does this do for you?

Brother: It brings order to the chaos of my head and brings to me a base of wisdom!

Coach: And what separation occurs for you as a result?

Brother: I separate myself from those who don't know them and who have not done the same.

Coach: Are you feeling lonely yet?

Brother: Not really.

Coach: Why?

Brother: Because by separating myself from those who do not know them, I join in on the fun that all those who do know them are having.

Coach: So, you separate yourself from the ignorant masses to become part of a group who is not ignorant by developing and refining your mental skills?

Brother: Yes. I earned membership in this group by doing the Work.

Coach: Agreed!

Brother: And if I take that information to the next level, I also separate myself from ruffians.

Coach: How so?

Brother: By bringing order to the chaos of both my head and heart and earning it, I don't ask for, demand or expect things that I have not earned.

Coach: So, you're the result of several separating processes?

Brother: Yes. And who I am and what I have become is the offspring of all that widowing.

Coach: A Widow's Son!

Brother: Agreed!

Coach: So, who is *"The Widow?"*

Brother: *"The Widow"* is not a *"Who!"*

Coach: What is it then?

Brother: *"The Widow"* is a process that males engage in to separate from things that hold them back and that keep them bound.

Coach: What does it enable them to do?

Brother: It enables each of them to be his own man, especially amongst Brothers.

Coach: Agreed!

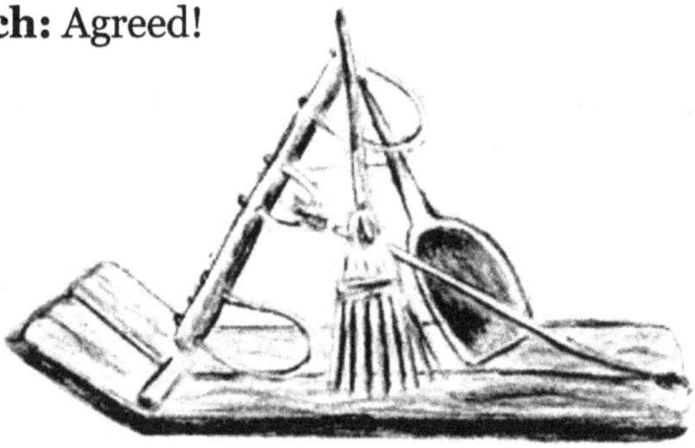

6. Denying Hiram

Let what you say be simply 'Yes' or 'No';
anything more than this comes from evil.
– Matthew 5:37

A Brother Asks: I noticed when Hiram was asked for secrets by the ruffians that he had three distinct ways of denying them. Is there something to this manner of denial that is not so obvious?

Coach: Obvious to whom?

Brother: Obvious to Brothers.

Coach: Do you mean the average Brother who has not done the Work, or to Brothers who have done the Work?

Brother: I mean to Brothers who have done the Work.

Coach: There's much revealed in his denial and it is obvious to Brothers who have done the Work. For those who have not done the Work, much is hidden in Hiram's denials.

Brother: Would you Work through them with me.

Coach: Sure! Where would you like to start?

Brother: How about the words used to deny the ruffians?

Coach: Great! So, what is one way that Hiram denies the ruffians?

Brother: When asked for the secrets, he says that he *"cannot"* provide them.

Coach: Yes, and another way?

Brother: When asked for the secrets a second time, he says that he *"shall not"* provide them.

Coach: Yes, and the last way?

Brother: When asked for the secrets a third time, he says that he *"will not"* provide them.

Coach: Okay. Put all three responses together.

Brother: I cannot. I shall not. I will not.

Coach: Yes. What pattern of denial are you seeing here?

Brother: I see three distinct communicated terms with three distinct messages.

Coach: And what are they?

Brother: The three terms used are *"cannot"*, *"shall not"* and *"will not."*

Coach: What does the first term tell you?

Brother: It tells me that Hiram is saying that what he is being asked for is impossible to provide. It simply cannot be done in actuality.

Coach: Agreed! And what is the second term being used?

Brother: The second term is *"shall not."*

Coach: What does that tell you?

Brother: The term *"shall not"* is a prescriptive obligator.

Coach: What does a prescriptive obligator do?

Brother: It obligates a person toward what is to become or what is to be done.

Coach: That is my understanding as well. What is Hiram denying the ruffians by using this term?

Brother: He is telling the ruffians that he cannot obligate himself to do something that is impossible to do.

Coach: I agree. Hiram, by virtue of it being impossible, concisely conveys that he is obligated to deny their request.

Brother: Agreed.

Coach: What about the third way he denies them?

Brother: He uses the term *"will not"* in his colloquies with them.

Coach: And what does the use of this phrase tell you?

Brother: It tells me that Hiram also had no desire to assist them in their efforts.

Coach: How so?

Brother: The use of the word *"will"* expresses desire. He stated that he *"will not"* provide them with what they ask. He desired not to help them.

Coach: Agreed! Please put it all together.

Brother: Hiram denies the ruffians in three distinct ways.

Coach: They are?

Brother: He tells them what they are asking for is impossible to deliver. He states they cannot prescribe impossible ends into existence. He also affirms that he has no desire to waste his time assisting them toward impossible ends.

Coach: Agreed! So, what's the lesson presented here?

Brother: Ah! The *"lesson."*

Coach: Yes, the lesson.

Brother: Based upon what is conveyed through allegory here, Beauty *cannot, shall not* and *will not* give up its secrets when there is a clear absence of wisdom and strength, much less the lack of agreement between the two.

Coach: It certainly seems this way.

Brother: What's more, it is impossible for Beauty to do so without the presence and agreement of all three!

Coach: Agreed!

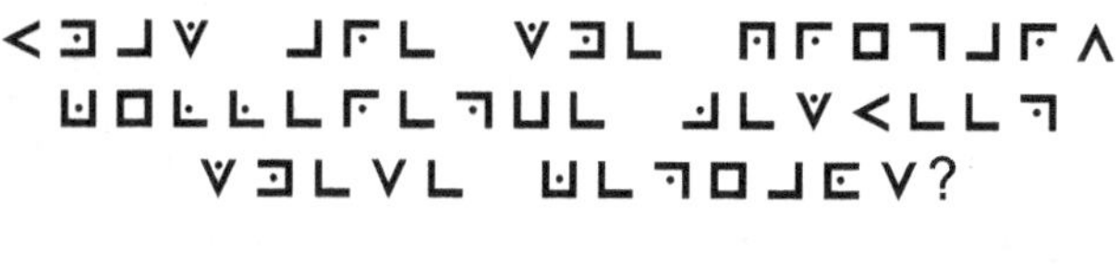

7. The Secrets

They know nothing, they understand nothing; their eyes are plastered over so they cannot see, and their minds closed so they cannot understand. – Isaiah 44:18

A Brother Asks: What can you tell me about the secrets that the ruffians sought?

Coach: That's a great question. What have you heard them to be?

Brother: I keep on hearing that it's the Master's Word that they sought.

Coach: Yes. I have heard similar. What else have you heard?

Brother: That they were also seeking the other secrets of a Master Mason.

Coach: I too recall hearing this.

Brother: But the emphasis that I hear is almost obsessively upon *"The Master's Word."*

Coach: You are not alone.

Brother: I've also been told that we're given *"The Master's Word"* when we go through specific higher degrees.

Coach: I have heard so as well.

Brother: But if all there is to getting The Master's Word is just going through another ceremony, then all a candidate has to do is simply pay another fee and go through another ceremony.

Coach: Yes, the operative phrase being, *"if all there is."* What are you getting at?

Brother: If Hiram is dead, how can The Master's word be provided to me just by taking another degree? That simply doesn't make any sense!

Coach: Yes. You are correct and you are not the first to come to that conclusion.

Brother: There's got to be more to it than just going through a ceremony and being told.

Coach: There is.

Brother: What's missing?

Coach: Part of the puzzle becomes clearer when you ask yourself what the reasons were behind seeking the secrets.

Brother: How do I find that out?

Coach: Reviewing ritual helps. They can be found in two distinct places.

Brother: Where are they found?

Coach: Within the third degree drama and the answer that an officer provides when asked why he became a Master Mason.

Brother: Okay. Thanks. I have them. The reasons are so that one could travel, work, earn, support and contribute masterfully.

Coach: Yes. That is what I understand to be the reasons.

Brother: So the ruffians were trying to get the secrets so that they could do all that? I take it that *"The Master's Word"* was a major part of these secrets.

Coach: That's my take on it.

Brother: But Hiram said that he *could not, should not and would not* provide it to them.

Coach: Yes. He did say these words.

Brother: So what are these secrets?

Coach: The key is found in what the secrets provide to the one who bears them.

Brother: Provide?

Coach: Yes, provide. The secrets provide the carrier with the ability to travel, work and earn master's wages. What allows for this?

Brother: Mastery, right?

Coach: That's my take on it.

Brother: But what does mastery have to do with a *"word?"*

Coach: That's the best question yet!

Brother: Why do you say this?

Coach: Because that question will lead you to The Word that so many seek.

Brother: Okay, so that question is a stepping stone to my goal?

Coach: Yes. Please, tell me what's required to have mastery?

Brother: Experience, skill development and artistic abilities.

Coach: Agreed! What triplet inculcated through ritual could be used to express the same three?

Brother: Wisdom is obtained through experience.

Coach: Yes, and?

Brother: Strength is obtained through skill development.

Coach: Without a doubt! And?

Brother: Beauty is obtained through artistic abilities.

Coach: It sounds like the very three things that have to come together for mastery to exist are wisdom, strength and beauty.

Brother: It does sound like that.

Coach: Where do we find wisdom, strength and beauty within the allegory?

Brother: They are represented by the three Grand Masters.

Coach: Yes, and all three were present within the allegory.

Brother: Well, at first, but some ruffians killed beauty.

Coach: Ruffians who lacked what?

Brother: Experience, skill development and artistic abilities.

Coach: And because they didn't have the three all present and all in agreement with each other, they could never obtain The Master's Word.

Brother: Wait! Is that why Hiram said that all must be present and all must agree?

Coach: What do you think?

Brother: It sure does make sense when I examine the allegory symbolically.

Coach: Me too!

Brother: But this means *"The Master's Word"* is *not* an actual *"word."*

Coach: Yes, it means that exactly! What else does it mean?

Brother: It means that *"The Master's Word"* is a metaphor.

Coach: A metaphor for what?

Brother: A metaphor for the experience, skill development and artistic abilities one obtains and puts into practice in Masterful ways.

Coach: And what are the ramifications of this?

Brother: That any word that you could say or write could never be The Master's Word.

Coach: Why?

Brother: Because Mastery that enables and empowers you to travel, work and earn at a master's level must be results driven. Words are not results; they are only potentials.

Coach: Agreed! What else?

Brother: This Master's Word can't possibly be handed from one person to another.

Coach: Why is that?

Brother: Because we all have our own experiences, skill development and artistic abilities and they are and shall always be uniquely our own.

Coach: How does this apply to the story?

Brother: Hiram could not possibly give the demanding ruffians his experience, skill development and artistic abilities.

Coach: Meaning?

Brother: The ruffians thought that a word could make them passable as masters, not realizing it was their own personal experiences, skill development and artistic abilities that made them potentially masterful.

Coach: Did they obtain experience, develop their skills and hone their artistic abilities?

Brother: It's obvious they didn't.

Coach: How so?

Brother: They didn't realize what The Master's Word actually was and sought it through means that were ultimately futile.

Coach: Agreed!

8. Rejecting Joppa

And the king said, "Hang him on that." So they hanged Haman on the gallows that he had prepared for Mordecai. Then the wrath of the king abated. – Esther 7:10

A Brother Asks: Why did the three ruffians go to Joppa[ii] to escape?

Coach: Were they not trying to get out of the area?

Brother: Well, yes. But they could have taken many different routes. A sea route does make sense, but there's got to be something more to it.

Coach: Yes. They could have and each would have presented its own challenges.

Brother: Yes. I get that. However, there has got to be a reason why they went toward Joppa.

Coach: There was, and it presents a certain poetic irony.

Brother: See! I knew you'd have some inside scoop on this.

Coach: Do you want to walk through it with me?

Brother: I sure do!

[ii] Also known as *"Jaffa"*, *"Japho"*, or *"Yafo."*

Coach: Good. Let's go back to the part of the story where they were placing demands upon and attacking Beauty.

Brother: Wait! What? When were the three ruffians placing demands upon and attacking Beauty.

Coach: It occurred just before Hiram Abiff's death.

Brother: I don't remember any of this. I do know that they placed demands upon and attacked Hiram. But when did this other assault and battery occur.

Coach: You seem not to have understood the point my Brother.

Brother: So it appears. What am I missing?

Coach: You're not missing anything. Everything is right before you – hidden in plain sight.

Brother: Okay. Help me make the connections, please.

Coach: What does Hiram Abiff represent?

Brother: He represents one of three Grand Masters.

Coach: What else?

Brother: The Grand Junior Warden.

Coach: And?

Brother: He represents *"Beauty."* Wait! The ruffians were placing demands upon and attacking Beauty! Okay! I got it.

Coach: Good! And what ultimately occurred?

Brother: They eventually killed him and buried him in the rubbish of the temple.

Coach: Great! Now, restate this using the word *"Beauty"* instead.

Brother: Okay. The three ruffians placed demands upon and attacked Beauty. This assault and battery led to Beauty being murdered and buried in rubbish.

Coach: Yes! Spot on!

Brother: But what does this have to do with Joppa?

Coach: Have you looked up what the word actually means?

Brother: Joppa?

Coach: Yes. Joppa.

Brother: No. Not yet. What would I find?

Coach: It has a few variations, all of which mean some aspect of *"Beauty."*

Brother: Joppa means *"Beauty?"*

Coach: Yes. It certainly does.

Brother: So, what you are telling me is that the ruffians assaulted, battered, killed and buried Beauty, traveled about forty miles to Beauty only to have Beauty reject them?

Coach: No. The allegory is telling us this. And there's more!

Brother: More?

Coach: Yes, more. Why were these ruffians rejected?

Brother: The sea captain would not allow them on board his ship because they didn't have King Solomon's passport.

Coach: Yes. But that is approaching it from a story level. What is the allegorical level?

Brother: What do you mean?

Coach: Hiram Abiff was an allegorical characterization of Beauty. What was King Solomon's allegorical characterization?

Brother: Oh! He was allegorical for Wisdom.

Coach: Yes. So, was it Solomon's passport that they lacked allegorically?

Brother: No. They lacked Wisdom's Passport! They lacked Wisdom and hence they were rejected by Beauty!

Coach: I agree! And it was not for lack of any Strength on their part. However...

Brother: Yes, they were willing to pay their way but they lacked Wisdom and hence no amount of resources, as in Strength, would allow them the Beauty.

Coach: And?

Brother: And that limited their travels.

Coach: Agreed! So, did you catch the irony?

Brother: Yes.

Coach: So, what is it?

Brother: The very thing that they assaulted, killed and buried eventually rejected them outright because they were unwise.

Coach: Yes! What is the light that this reveals?

Brother: Without Wisdom, Strength alone, even when offered in the form of bribery money, is not enough to obtain Beauty's Secrets.

Coach: And?

Brother: Without Wisdom, Beauty will eventually reject you.

Coach: Agreed!

┘┘⊓>V ⊐⊓< ⅂┘⅂Λ ⅂□⊏LV ⊔□⊔
V⊐L ⌐>⊑⊑□┘⅂V ⊐┘>L V⊓ V⌐┘>L⊏
V⊓ ⊐LV V⊓ □⊓⊓⊓┘?

9. Ethiopia

The topaz of Ethiopia cannot equal it, nor can it be valued in pure gold. – Job 28:19

A Brother Asks: Why were the ruffians trying to get to Ethiopia?[5]

Coach: Why not?

Brother: But it doesn't make any sense[6].

Coach: What doesn't make sense?

Brother: Ethiopia in the time of King Solomon was a powerful kingdom and in alliance with him.

Coach: And you're implying that such a kingdom would not be a good place for murderers to take refuge?

Brother: Yes! That's exactly what I am implying.

Coach: Have you taken into account that ruffians don't listen?

Brother: Of course they don't listen? What do ruffians not listening have to do with trying to figure out why they were trying to get to Ethiopia?

Coach: First of all, are you assuming that I am talking about the ruffians within story?

Brother: Well of course I am. What other ruffians could there be?

Coach: Great question! There are two sets of ruffians here.

Brother: Two? Are you referring to all the Fellow Crafts within the story being divided into those who are reformed and those who are unreformed?

Coach: No. I am not.

Brother: Then I have no clue as to what you are referring. Please explain your comment.

Coach: Okay. There are the ruffians within the ritual story.

Brother: Yes.

Coach: This includes all the Fellow Crafts involved, whether they participated directly or indirectly in the plot to obtain the secrets.

Brother: Understood.

Coach: Then there are the other ruffians who try to figure out what the story means.

Brother: Oh! I had not considered that as an option.

Coach: Many within the Craft do not.

Brother: Are you implying that the ruffians who try to figure out the story are not making some vital connection?

Coach: I am implying that exactly.

Brother: What vital connection are they not making?

Coach: The vital connection is simple. The three ruffians responsible for the murder were not trying to get to Ethiopia.

Brother: What?

Coach: Yes. They were merely trying to get as far away as possible in an effort to outrun their accountability.

Brother: But the ship captain said he was bound for Ethiopia.

Coach: Yes. You are correct. It was the ship captain who said that he was bound for Ethiopia.

Brother: Wait! Are you saying that it was never the ruffians' intent to go to Ethiopia?

Coach: Yes. That is what I am saying. Their sole intent was to leave the country. Joppa was one of many routes. It was only after the ship's captain revealed to them where he was bound that they told him that his destination was theirs as well.

Brother: That would mean that what they were trying to do is get out of the area as fast as they could and that Ethiopia was merely the ship captain's destination.

Coach: Yes!

Brother: This would mean that they were waiting for the captain to tell them where he was going before they told him that his destination was where they were heading too.

Coach: Yes! This is the vital information that many ruffians don't glean when they ask the question, *"Why Ethiopia?"*

Brother: And now that I can make the vital connection I know the answer.

Coach: Which is?

Brother: Why Ethiopia? It was the destination that the ship captain was heading. If they wanted to continue their swift exodus by way of that ship, they would have had to say that Ethiopia was where they also wanted to go. It would be where they would wind up if they obtained passage and travelled all the way!

Coach: Yes. It was not something that they intentionally pursued. It was merely a destination where they would have found themselves had they had Wisdom's passport.

Brother: Okay, I get it. The ruffians were not deliberately trying to get to Ethiopia. Ethiopia became their destination only after the ship's captain told them where he was going.

Coach: Yes.

Brother: Furthermore, just because they got on a ship that was going there, doesn't mean they couldn't have gotten off that ship along the route.

Coach: Absolutely! The ship's destination was set. The ruffians could have changed their destination anywhere along the way.

Brother: But this raises a question?

Coach: What's that?

Brother: Why was the destination part of ritual?

Coach: Which ritual?

Brother: Freemasonic ritual!

Coach: It is only part of some rituals. It is found within most of the USA and some Scottish ritual systems, along with a few spread out over the globe. However, it is not universal.

Brother: When did its use begin?

Coach: As in, when was it added to ritual?

Brother: Okay, yes. When did it first appear?

Coach: It appeared in USA ritual only after the ruffian's names first appeared.

Brother: When did the ruffian's names first appear?

Coach: In 1760.

Brother: Do you think there might be a connection?

Coach: There could be.

Brother: Care to share a few?

Coach: Sure. I have two. The book of Enoch was rediscovered by Scottish Brother James Bruce and brought back to Europe around 1765. It caused quite a stir.

Brother: What's the connection?

Coach: It is cannon in the Ethiopian Bible, and Ethiopia is where he obtained it.

Brother: Interesting! What's more?

Coach: The Book of Jubilees is also part of the Ethiopian Bible .

Brother: So?

Coach: It is thought by some that the name *"Jubilees"* is close enough to the ruffian names that it warranted an addition of an Ethiopian destination to stir curiosity and adventure.

Brother: Did it?

Coach: For those who desired it, yes!

Brother: This is all conjecture is it not?

Coach: Yes. However, trying to solve such a mystery brings about honed researching skills that are very valuable to those who seek light.

Brother: Okay. I understand. Ritual is a seventeenth century version of our current hyperlinked documents.

Coach: How so?

Brother: The words and phrases used within our rituals are there to lead us to further learning, investigation, and discoveries. Should we use them as subtle or deliberate prompts for further exploration and study, we accomplish this.

Coach: Absolutely! Those who understand this open up whole worlds of learning, investigation, and discoveries for themselves and others.

Brother: Meaning?

Coach: They become travelling men.

10. Wayfaring

A highway will be there, a roadway, And it will be called the Highway of Holiness; The unclean will not travel on it. But it will be for him who walks that way. And fools will not wander on it.
– Isaiah 35:8

A Brother Asks: What significance does the character of the Wayfaring Man have to the candidate?

Coach: It is a clever allusion to a *"Traveling*[7] *Man"* that appears in some USA rituals[8] with all its implications. It is not universally present in all rituals.

Brother: Allusion?

Coach: Yes, it alludes, as in, it *"indirectly refers"*, to something of which the candidate should be aware as to his current state of being.

Brother: What does this have to do with a Traveling Man?

Coach: A Wayfarer is a Traveler, one who likely uses roads and paths and usually travels them on foot.

Brother: So, you're telling me that the candidate should know that the wayfaring man is a traveler, who likely travels on foot and uses roads or paths?

Coach: Yes.

Brother: That's it?

Coach: No, there's more.

Brother: Okay... what are the implications?

Coach: I'll redirect your question toward another: With what is the term *"wayfarer"* associated?

Brother: Researching it further, I found that the term *"wayfarer"* is associated with *"becoming"* as in, someone who has yet to arrive at either a destination or comprehension.

Coach: What does using the term within the third degree tell the candidate?

Brother: That the use of the term *"wayfarer"* within ritual is to let the candidate know that he has not yet arrived or become what he has set out to do, or, in a more personal way, it tells him that he does not fully comprehend what has been offered him?

Coach: Exactly! To what else does it allude?

Brother: If I were to take the aspect of usual application, a wayfaring man is one that makes it to his destination by taking the necessary steps to get there.

Coach: Meaning?

Brother: He himself does whatever Work is required to get him to where he wants to go. No one travels for him or carries him along.

Coach: Agreed!

11. The Fifteen Ruffians

When God saw their deeds, that they turned from their wicked way, then God relented concerning the calamity which He had declared He would bring upon them. And He did not do it. – Jonah 3:10

Brother: Were the remaining twelve[9] Fellow Crafts reformed ruffians?[10]

Coach: Before I respond directly to your question, let me take some liberty here and lay a foundation for my response.

Brother: Okay.

Coach: Freemasonry does not make good men better.

Brother: Wait! What?

Coach: That phrase is a fabricated slogan that serves the purpose of gaining the interest of a target market. It has worked unbelievably well over the years and is well suited to that purpose.

Brother: Please explain how you arrived at this conclusion.

Coach: Sure. If you inspect the actual results of Craft influence upon its members and do so in an unbiased way, it should become obvious from the clear evidence that it is only by seeking and practicing Masonry, *not just Freemasonry*, that a Good Man becomes a Better Man.

Brother: Okay, you're differentiating the membership development aspects from the personal development aspects?

Coach: Yes. The organization educates its members to become better so that it gets the support it needs to continue. It does not educate these members directly towards become better men.

Brother: Understood.

Coach: That being said, let's take a closer look at this.

Brother: Yes. Let's do just that.

Coach: We already know that Mainstream Freemasonry is an organization of men who collectively claim that they seek to make Good Men Better.

Brother: Yes. It certainly does this.

Coach: It also lays claim to be supporting this end without wavering.

Brother: Agreed!

Coach: It does this by directing members' attention toward focusing upon those things that each can do to improve themselves.

Brother: Yes. That direction is inculcated each time ritual is performed.

Coach: Yes. It does this in the hope that members may eventually come to know and embrace the personal development Work; not just organizational support activities.

Brother: So, where are these two disconnected?

Coach: To be valid, these claims must be backed by action on the part of each member for that Betterment to be realized.

Brother: How does this occur?

Coach: The first step toward that end is taken when members realize and understand that there actually is a difference between the actions that support the organization and the actions that support the betterment that it espouses.

Brother: Is there a second step?

Coach: Yes. The second step toward that end is realizing and understanding that participation in organizational activities is not the same as doing the betterment work that it espouses; these are two entirely different activities and they serve two entirely different ends.

Brother: What are those ends?

Coach: Organizational ends are activities directed toward keeping the machine running.

Brother: And what are the ends of betterment?

Coach: Betterment ends are those activities designed to bring about maturity and masterful skills of members as human beings, no matter where they go or what system or organization they participate within.

Brother: I see two entirely different ends in what you describe. Organization's ends support activities that make for better members.

Betterment ends support activities that make good men better.

Coach: Yes. Should members get upset or offended by this information?

Brother: Only if they stubbornly insist upon not earnestly examining what betterment of one's self actually entails.

Coach: Agreed! Now that this foundation has been laid, let's get back to your question.

Brother: Good!

Coach: I believe deeply that the twelve Fellow Crafts who went back to Work were more heroic than any other characters within the Temple's Allegorical Tale.

Brother: How so?

Coach: Taking up the Work of betterment with an unwavering intent to complete it within one's lifetime is one of the most heroic and noblest of journeys any man can undertake.

Brother: I understand, although I had not looked at it from that vantage point before this conversation.

Coach: It takes some deep perpending to grasp such an insight.

Brother: Thanks.

Coach: But don't relax just yet. It takes more than you just understanding.

Brother: What more does it take?

Coach: Great question. You must also recognize this need to improve and then take the necessary steps to dedicate yourself to its fulfillment and completion.

Brother: This is truly a rare and noble quality.

Coach: Yes.

Brother: How did you come to know all this?

Coach: I know from experience what it actually takes and what occurs when it is not completed.

Brother: What does it take?

Coach: A man must cultivate something very special and utterly unique within himself to take upon himself such Work and then move it toward completion.

Brother: What result can he expect?

Coach: Transformation! The Work *transforms* the man, his life and his world.

Brother: I take it that this Work is not for wimps, wusses, or ruffians (those who ruff)[iii].

Coach: Yes. It is not and especially these. And therein lays the answer to your question.

Brother: Do you mean the original question I asked about the twelve Fellow Craft being reformed ruffians?

[iii] **Ruff**: an archaic term meaning to *"trump"*; not follow suit; skip over what is usually necessary and required to accomplish desired ends.

Coach: Yes. The twelve Fellow Crafts were part of the original conspiracy to ruff, as in, not follow suit on doing the required Work.

Brother: Ruff? As in, not following suit and completing it?

Coach: Yes. They had every intention to ruff. They were not going to follow through, but, ultimately, they changed their minds.

Brother: They decided to do the Work?

Coach: Yes. They followed suit on pursuing and completing the Work they had promised to complete.

Brother: This is an interesting way of looking at this.

Coach: Thanks.

Brother: So where does this leave the twelve Fellow Crafts?

Coach: Well, some Craft members facetiously claim that only three of the Fellow Crafts actually returned to King Solomon after successfully apprehending those who killed the Grand Master. They also say the rest of them are still wandering. A quick review reveals this cannot be so.

Brother: Why?

Coach: We are left with a distinct understanding that all twelve decided not to go along with the three wayward killers' plans. They planned to reform their ways and get back to the business of doing the Work to complete the temple.

Brother: I sense there is more.

Coach: Yes, there is. Even though they may not have officially reported back within the allegory's script, they all participated in raising Beauty out of the grave at the end of the tale.

Brother: So, then you are saying that the twelve Fellow Craft were reformed ruffians?

Coach: The story is conveying this. They were reformed ruffians in as much as we are left with the impression at the end that they were following suit and doing the necessary Work.

Three Blind Men,
Three Blind Men
See How they Ruff,
See How they Ruff!

They Ruffed right after
The Master's Word.
And Misunderstood what
Remained Unheard.

Have you ever Seen
Such Ignorance Assured
As Three Blind Men?

12. Spotting Craft Ruffians

God hands me over to ruffians, and tosses me into the hands of the wicked. – Job 16:11

A Brother Asks: Coach! I'm a bit frustrated and hurting. I don't like what I'm seeing in and what I'm getting from some of my Brothers. Could you give me a quick guide? How can I spot Craft Ruffians?

Coach: Let me respond by providing you a quick and easy to use list of behaviors you can use to assess your Brothers should you want to identify them as Ruffians.

The Short List[11] for *"You might be dealing with a Ruffian Brother when he ..."*

1. ... Inaccurately or purposely misrepresents a Brother, his activities, and results.
2. ... Bears false witness and intentionally misquotes a Brother's words so that they reflect poorly upon that Brother.
3. ... Maligns, Misrepresents or Vilifies a Brother's intentions.
4. ... Indignantly condemns a Brother's Work.
5. ... Sabotages a Brother's pursuits and endeavors and the support that others might provide him.
6. ... Attacks, Belittles and Berates the institutions and faiths with which a Brother is associated.

7. ... Slanders a Brother's education as being suspect and false and not what he would choose for himself.
8. ... Misleads others about a Brother based upon his own conjectures.
9. ... Silently and Continuously Endorses the Assassination of a Brother's character.
10. ... Purposefully deals with a Brother indirectly, deceitfully so and with malicious intent masked in righteousness.
11. ... Encourages and Endorses Social Pressures Intended to Sway Brothers toward his will and pleasure by manipulating those who surround and influence his target.
12. ... Assures Brothers, by what he says and through what he does, that he means others harm and he does so beyond any shadow of a heartfelt doubt.

13. Symbolic Penalties

And Cain said, "My punishment is greater than my strength." – Genesis 4:13

Brother: What does a Brother have to do to suffer the Penalties of his Obligation?

Coach: Great question! Would you like to work through them with me?

Brother: Absolutely!

Coach: Good! A Brother suffers the first penalty whenever his words prove to have no Value.

Brother: What makes a man's words valueless?

Coach: His contrary actions.

Brother: Contrary actions?

Coach: Yes. His contrary actions shall eventually cause every person with integrity to ignore his words.

Brother: That makes sense. Those actions render his tongue useless.

Coach: And what occurs when his tongue is useless?

Brother: There would be no need to have that tongue at all.

Coach: I agree. And how does a man suffer when others have judged his tongue to be useless?

Brother: He will not be taken seriously. They shall no longer invest in the words that come from his mouth.

Coach: What is the likelihood of such a man being believed?

Brother: It is highly unlikely. It would be as if his tongue were no longer there.

Coach: Agreed!

Brother: What about the second penalty?

Coach: A Brother suffers the second penalty when his heart is shown not to be in what he is doing.

Brother: How can you tell?

Coach: You can tell by the manner he involves himself in what he is doing and whether he is invested in his work or not.

Brother: What occurs when he is not invested in his Work?

Coach: His lack of investment directly affects the quality of his results.

Brother: And what does this do to his heart?

Coach: It renders his Heart useless.

Brother: Agreed! How does he suffer though?

Coach: He shall be excluded. No one will involve him in their serious activities since it is obvious to all that whatever he does will be render heartless results.

Brother: What about the third penalty?

Coach: A Brother suffers the third penalty when his Head and his Heart are shown to be torn in two different directions.

Brother: This makes sense.

Coach: How so?

Brother: I've seen men emotionally, intellectually and spiritually pulled apart when their head and heart were not aligned or in agreement with each other.

Coach: They are severed in twain?

Brother: And pulled in two different directions!

Coach: How useful are such men to others or themselves?

Brother: For all intents and purposes, they are rendered useless.

Coach: How do such men suffer?

Brother: Some suffer mental and emotional anguish caused by them being severed in twain. Others suffer the same by being severed from relationships damaged by their condition.

Brother: I'm seeing that although these penalties are put forth as symbolic, they have real life consequences.

Coach: They sure do! Although each is presented as *only symbolic*, each penalty is allegorical for the reality that is self-inflicted by the person who violates his Obligations.

Brother: Coach, let's make this personal.

Coach: Okay. Why were they revealed to you?

Brother: They were revealed to me so that I would know what occurs by my own hand should I manifest specific conditions.

Coach: Agreed. What is the first condition?

Brother: When my Words and Deeds are without Integrity, my words and actions cannot be trusted.

Coach: Yes! What is the second condition?

Brother: When my Heart is uninvolved, I am not invested in what I do. My heart and work results cannot be trusted.

Coach: Agreed! What is the third condition?

Brother: When my Head and Heart are in Conflict, my house is divided and I'm torn in two. I cannot be trusted.

Coach: What pattern are you seeing in all this?

Brother: It's clear that men who suffer the first penalty shall no longer be listened to and no one shall place any value in their words.

Coach: Are you telling me that his words shall have no weight and they shall not be taken seriously.

Brother: I am. Others will know better than to listen to such a man. The world shall shun him as a man unable to speak with Integrity.

Coach: Anything to add to this?

Brother: Yes. When a man's heart has been proven not to be involved in what he does, anything he might commit to or be involved in will clearly be done in a heartless manner.

Coach: Will others no longer place their trust in him?

Brother: They will not, unless they are fools. They will know better than to have him involved or to take serious anything to which he commits.

Coach: It sounds like the World will shun him as a man whose Heart is not involved.

Brother: Yes. Furthermore, the world will no longer invest in such a man when he reveals his head and heart to be in conflict with each other and that he's being pulled in two entirely different directions.

Coach: Are you saying that the world will shun him as a man unable to be totally invested due to his lack of integrity and his torn being?

Brother: I am saying just that.

Coach: Would you say this plainly and personally?

Brother: Sure! When I violate my obligations, I *self-impose* any one of the three penalties upon my person. No one else is involved. They don't have to be. I do all the work myself and upon myself.

Coach: What is the impact upon others?

Brother: Others are impacted negatively by my violations and they will not want any part of my future impacts.

Coach: How's this hitting you?

Brother: It's a harsh reality. But it's also clear that by honoring my obligations, I can avoid all this.

Coach: That's the truth. It is most unfortunate that both insiders and outsiders to the Craft have no idea that these realities are what are meant by the phrase *"only symbolic."*

Brother: *"Only symbolic"* doesn't mean that they are not pointing toward real consequences associated with metaphorical conveyances.

Coach: Agreed. Far too many people are symbolically illiterate. They take allegorical, symbolic and metaphorical conveyances as literal and not figurative, as allegory is meant to be taken.

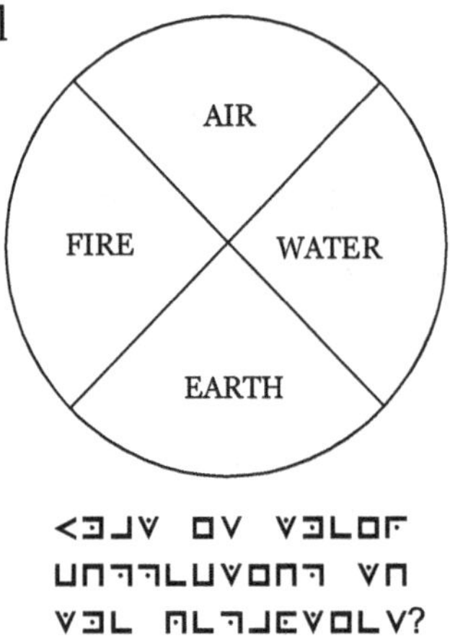

Brother: Yes. As a result of this manner, we have entire cross-sections of our society being swept away in ignorant conclusions and actions that have no basis in reality or our Craft.

Coach: Yes. Unfortunately, yes.

14. Cowan & Ruffian Insights

"The pride of thine heart hath deceived thee, thou that dwellest in the clefts of the rock, whose habitation is high; that saith in his heart, 'Who shall bring me down to the ground?' Though thou exalt thyself as the eagle, and though thou set thy nest among the stars, thence will I bring thee down, saith the Lord." – Obadiah 1:3-4

A Brother Asks: Does ritual provide any insights into cowans and ruffians?

Coach: Ritual alludes to many things. You're better off using it as a springboard from which to investigate these allusions further.

Brother: Okay. Where can I start?

Coach: Great question. Mind if I get a little poetic in my responses?

Brother: Not at all.

Coach: Good. Ritual is truly subtle.

Brother: I'll say it is.

Coach: Its soft embrace cleverly disguises many nuances unseen by those who seek them not.

Brother: And there are many who don't.

Coach: Agreed. Returning its embrace often brings forth light hidden by the shadows of ignorance. When you seek the nuances, you shall find wonders.

Brother: Agreed!

Coach Sometimes it's the little things that go unnoticed, until they begin to irritate you.

Brother: Like?

Coach: Here's an example. This occurred for me recently when I was tickled in a most annoying way by the phrase, *"cleft of the rocks."*

Brother: What happened?

Coach: I didn't know why it kept fluttering under my nose, but it was clear that it was not going away on its own.

Brother: What did you do?

Coach: After numerous unwanted assaults, I finally took mindful notice of it and grabbed hold.

Brother: What did you grasp?

Coach: As I did, I was reminded that I was a Mason *and I Work on Rocks*. This hard reminder compelled me to look up the word, *"cleft"*[12] to obtain a more solid understanding. *I'm glad I did!*

Brother: What did you find?

Coach: Upon its examination, I connected further to subtle allusions within ritual.

Brother: And?

Coach: There was the obvious connection to the ruffians who were hiding in the *cleft of the rocks*.

Brother: I have thought about that before. What other connections did you make?

Coach: There was a connection to the existing *hollows* where our heels find solace as we progress from candidate to Master.

Brother: That's one I had not thought of.

Coach: There was also the not so common connection to the now obsolete meaning of the word, *"cowan"*, that meant at one time *"hollow, gap, crevice, indent or hole."*

Brother: I want to perpend that one for sure.

Coach: That one matter continued to roll around within my mind as I found more associated allusions and connections.

Brother: What did you do next?

Coach: When I laid each of them out upon my working slab, I had a profound insight.

Brother: What was that?

Coach: *These Allusions all point to Unfinished Work!*

Brother: That makes sense.

Coach: I'm glad you sense this. Masons are *told* that specific Work must be completed to achieve Mastery.

Brother: Agreed!

Coach: That Work is clearly implied by ritual, but the Work is not the ritual itself.

Brother: Understood.

Coach: Even the Third Degree Allegory directs us back to completing that Work.

Brother: I'm sure the third degree does far more than that.

Coach: Yes, it does! This allegory also warns us about making any effort to dismiss any Work.

Brother: In what way?

Coach: Ritual tells us through Allusion that, when our Work remains unfinished, our *Word's Value* is ripped from us, our *Desires* become fodder for beasts and fowl and our very *Being* is torn in two differing directions;

Brother: I take it that these allusions and warnings are not gleaned by many Brothers initially.

Coach: Yes. Few Brothers heed such warnings.

Brother: Even fewer heed them long term.

Coach: Agreed. Ritual tells us how to recognize them though. Their very looks betray them!

Brother: But how?

Coach: Great question! Let's review this!

Brother: Okay:

Coach: Ritual tells us that we can recognize Cowanistic members[13] by their unfinished Work.

Brother: Can you provide some examples?

Coach: Sure. The hollows of their feet are only used as resting places for heels that have yet to walk the path.

Brother: Are you referring to the steps, the heels and the hollows used within ritual?

Coach: Yes, I am. Furthermore, you'll always see gaps in their Work.

Brother: Ah! Cowans! The cracks, hollows and indents formed by unsquared Work.

Coach: Yes. It is not their concern though.

Brother: Why is this so?

Coach: Cowans remain steadfastly complacent 1) to progress no further than they desire to, and 2) to receive less for unfinished Work.

Brother: How do Cowans compare to ruffians?

Coach: Ruffian Brothers are quite a different matter.

Brother: How so?

Coach: Let's take a look at Time, as in the use of their twenty-four inch gauge.

Brother: Okay, let's!

Coach: Ruffians desperately want what they have yet to earn but they are unwilling to put the time in to earn it.

Brother: I can see this. What about Morality, as in the use of the square?

Coach: Ruffians feel entitled to more than they deserve and they try to dishonestly receive it. The truth is this, they are unwilling to Work legitimately to earn what they desire.

Brother: I had not thought of it this way before.

Coach: You are not alone. Far too many have not thought it through as you just have.

Brother: What about completing things, as in using the setting maul to put things to rest?

Coach: Ruffians' Ashlars are wholly divided.

Brother: Ah! Their entire being is *"Severed in Twain!"*

Coach: Yes! They are recognized by their arrogance – they believe the rules do not apply to them – but more so by the cleft in their Ashlars, where you shall find their true selves hiding.

Brother: That's quite an image you paint.

Coach: Thanks. It's truly amazing the insights you can glean when you take a crack at probing what irritates you.

Brother: I see this. Sometimes you get to view new holes.

Coach: Yes. Though every time you do, you get whole new views!

15. Ruffian Symbolism

For it is written, "I will destroy the wisdom of the wise, and the intelligence of the intelligent I will confound." – 1 Corinthians 1:19

A Brother Asks: Are there hidden symbolisms being conveyed through the names of the three ruffians?

Coach: Yes; there are several.

Brother: Would you take me through them.

Coach: Sure. Please keep in mind we do this premised upon their names intentionally being contrived to convey symbolic meanings.

Brother: Understood.

Coach: Let's start by examining the differences and commonalities between the names.

Brother: Okay. It's obvious they all share in common the first five letters. It's the suffix of each of their names, the "*a*", "*o*", and "*um*", that differ.

Coach: Yes.

Brother: But to what do they allude?

Coach: That's a great question. What have you come up with so far?

Brother: Your use of the word "*suffix*" is interesting. I was thinking along that line when I first encountered them.

Coach: Where did this lead you?

Brother: I was leaning toward Latin and how the endings of words change to denote gender and tense within context.

Coach: And did that get you anywhere?

Brother: Yes. It drove me to the point of frustration.

Coach: How so?

Brother: I was unable to discern any recognizable pattern to it.

Coach: You are not alone. Brothers with even rudimentary knowledge of Latin have tried the routes you've taken and have come up with nothing substantial, other than their own frustrations to account for their efforts. Well, that and a better understanding of how Latin suffixes work.

Brother: Okay, so I am not alone in this directional effort.

Coach: You are not alone my Brother.

Brother: So what other directions can I explore?

Coach: Look at the tales' clues.

Brother: Clues?

Coach: Yes. Look at the clues sprinkled throughout the story and look toward what connections they allude.

Brother: For instance?

Coach: You know Hiram was in what phase of his life within the story?

Brother: He was older, so that would mean he was in *"age."*

Coach: Yes. And in relation to the seasons, to what season does *"age"* allude?

Brother: Fall or autumn.

Coach: Yes! What are the fall constellations?

Brother: Let's see... there are Libra, Scorpio, and Sagittarius.

Coach: Yes, and what are the last letters of each of these constellation names?

Brother: I get *"a"*, *"o"* and *"us"*, if I were to take it that you were trying to draw a correlation to the names of the ruffians.

Coach: I certainly am. What are you gathering by this information?

Brother: That the Ruffian name endings allude to the constellations of autumn?

Coach: Yes.

Brother: But the last ruffian's name ends in *"um"*, not *"us."*

Coach: Agreed. However, have you checked out how these constellations are spelled in Latin?

Brother: When I do, I get Libra, Scorpio, and Sagittarium, and the name endings of the constellations match perfectly with that of the ruffian's name endings!

Coach: Yes. They do match! What is this information telling those who have taken the time to examine the allegory?

Brother: That in the autumn of a man's life, he'll see representatives of the Fall Constellations?

Coach: Yes. And which Constellation is the beginning of a man's autumn?

Brother: The beginning of a man's autumn is Libra.

Coach: And which of the ruffian's correspond to Libra?

Brother: The first ruffian.

Coach: And with what working tool did he attacked Hiram?

Brother: In the most common American Rite, he used the twenty-four inch gauge.

Coach: What is the use of the twenty-four inch gauge?

Brother: To measure and manage time?

Coach: So, it is a time management tool to which Hiram was attacked?

Brother: Yes. I'm beginning to see a connection.

Coach: What connection are you seeing?

Brother: That the first ruffian represents a person who does not effectively deal with time.

Coach: And?

Brother: The mismanagement of time wounded Hiram.

Coach: Did he survive?

Brother: Yes. And I can see how this applies.

Coach: How so?

Brother: As disciplined as Hiram was in managing his time, he was still impacted negatively by the mismanagement and lack of discipline of others.

Coach: Yes. What does the story tell us next?

Brother: Soon thereafter he was confronted by the second ruffian.

Coach: And what part of a man's autumn did this ruffian represent?

Brother: The middle.

Coach: And the constellation?

Brother: Scorpio

Coach: With what working tool did he attack Hiram?

Brother: In the most common American Rite, he used the square.

Coach: What is the use of the Square?

Brother: To assure Work is Right or to make it Right when it is not.

Coach: To what else does the square allude?

Brother: A man's morality?

Coach: And when that square is linked to a man's morality, how is it referred?

Brother: The Square of Virtue?

Coach: Yes. How would an immoral or non-virtuous man use his square?

Brother: Abusively.

Coach: Was Hiram abused by the misuse of this working tool by another?

Brother: Yes. I can see how this applies.

Coach: How so?

Brother: As virtuous and moral as Hiram was, he was still impacted by the immorality and weaknesses of others.

Coach: Agreed! What does the tale tell us occurred next?

Brother: He was soon thereafter confronted by the third ruffian.

Coach: What part of a man's autumn did this ruffian represent?

Brother: The end.

Coach: What is the end of a Man's autumn?

Brother: The winter solstice or death.

Coach: Yes. What is the constellation?

Brother: Sagittarius, or in Latin, Sagitterium

Coach: Good! With what working tool did he attack Hiram?

Brother: The setting maul.

Coach: What is the use of the Setting Maul?

Brother: To drive ashlars into their proper place.

Coach: To what else does the setting maul allude?

Brother: A man's properly and patiently putting the finishing touches on his Work and more importantly, in the case of age, his life?

Coach: Yes. How would an impatient man use his setting maul?

Brother: With frustration driven by uncaring fervor.

Coach: Was Hiram abused by the misuse of this working tool by another?

Brother: Yes. I can see how this applies.

Coach: How so?

Brother: Although Hiram was patient and caring, he was still impacted by the impatience and uncaring of others.

Coach: Agreed!

Brother: But can't this also be taken personally too?

Coach: Yes, it can. Would you be so kind as to personalize all three ruffian attacks?

Brother: Sure! The first tool is about the demands of time. You must learn to deal effectively with the demands of time when you want Mastery.

Coach: Agreed! What about the next tool?

Brother: The second tool is about your own virtue and morality. You must develop both of these or your life and mastery will be held back by your weaknesses.

Coach: Yes! What about the third tool?

Brother: The third tool is about putting things to rest. This includes both your life's work and yourself. You must work in such a disciplined way as to make sure you don't ruin what you are trying to finish by being impatient and uncaring.

Coach: Agreed!

Brother: I have but one more question about the names.

Coach: And that is?

Brother: How much of this symbolism you're sharing is trying to make sense of names that may not have any basis in fact.

Coach: All of it.

Brother: All of it?

Coach: Yes, all of it.

Brother: Please explain.

Coach: The names of the ruffians first appeared in print in 1760. Prior to that, there is no record of their names ever being used in their present forms.

Brother: I sense there is more to this that you have just revealed.

Coach: There is.

Brother: Please tell!

Coach: The names as they appear in their current form are phonetic representations of what society members thought they heard during ritual performances. Most Brothers truly do not know the actual spelling of their names or what these phonetic representations actually allude.

Brother: What does that mean?

Coach: It means any explanation offered by most Brothers attempting to make either sense or utility of these phonetic representations is merely doing so to add some value to what has been overwhelmingly accepted and standardized by the Craft without question, in only some areas.

Brother: Some areas?

Coach: Yes. In some area rituals, there are no references to ruffians or their respective names. Instead of ruffians, there are only references to unnamed assassins.

Brother: Thanks for sharing honestly on this.

Coach: You are most welcome.

┌>└VVV V⊐┘┌⊓└┐ V⊏□⊏⊏V <⊐└┐ V┘⊏└┐.

16. Ruffian Meaning

Come, let us go down, and there confound their language, that they may not understand one another's speech. – Genesis 11:7

A Brother Asks: Are there hidden meanings[14] being conveyed within the names of the three ruffians?

Coach: There sure are!

Brother: Wow! You didn't hesitate at all in replying.

Coach: That's because there is no hesitation in my answer.

Brother: What makes you so confident in your response?

Coach: I've done the Work my Brother.

Brother: What can you tell me then?

Coach: I can tell you from the start that I was ignorant of and naive to their actual meanings since the beginning of my travels.

Brother: What else?

Coach: These same conditions have existed within the craft for over two hundred years.

Brother: Why over two hundred years?

Coach: Because just over two hundred years ago the ruffians' names first appeared in print.

Brother: Where did their names appear in print?

Coach: In a book published in London in 1760.[15]

Brother: And their names didn't appear prior to that?

Coach: Yes. Prior to that, no publicly disclosed English writings reflected any ruffian name or information other than that there were three of them and they were referred to as ruffians or assassins.

Brother: What makes you so confident that you know the meanings of the ruffians' names?

Coach: I have done the Work.

Brother: What Work is that?

Coach: The Work of the Apprentice and Fellow Craft.

Brother: How did that Work help you?

Coach: It helped me recognize that all the other theories, speculations and conjectures were off in their premises.[16]

Brother: What premises where they?

Coach: One was that the ruffian's names were possibly related to and variants of the Hebrew word *"Jubilee."*[17]

Brother: Is this true?

Coach: No. And then there is another premise that it came from a corruption of the word, *"Ghiblim"*, which supposedly means "*stonecutters*" or "*masons*" that were of the Fellow Craft class.

Brother: Is this true?

Coach: It is not, even though much verbiage has been put forth to show their possible connection and possible gradual transformations.

Brother: Then, what can you tell me?

Coach: The real meanings of their names are known and so is the story of the discovery of their meanings.

Brother: And?

Coach: And it is far less elaborate than others, but it is still pretty extraordinary.

Brother: Do tell and do not leave out a thing!

Coach: I'm glad that you are interested in the background.

Brother: I am, please, continue.

Coach: It started a little while back while I was listening to the video of a professor relaying a story of an incident between him and a few Canadian children who were three to four years of age.

Brother: Where was he at this time?

Coach: He was in his back yard building a fence. These children came up to him and he offered the hammer he was using to the oldest of them to handle and get a feel for it.

Brother: What happened?

Coach: He said the oldest blurted out in Joual[18] something that loosely translates to *"I'll steal that!"*

Brother: What made that so interesting?

Coach: When the professor tried to repeat back what the child said in this dialect of Quebec French, I was startled.

Brother: What did he say?

Coach: I thought he said, *"Jubela."*

Brother: What?

Coach: Yes! That's exactly what I said to myself when I first heard him say this.

Brother: What did you do?

Coach: I rewound and listened to the video several times in disbelief.

Brother: And?

Coach: Each time I heard it exactly the same. I was in a bit in shock but far more excited.

Brother: I can imagine! What did you do next?

Coach: I thought to myself, *"what if the ruffian's names were French in origin"* and immediately went to a translation program and keyed in, *"I'll steal that."*

Brother: What did it give back to you?

Coach: Nothing but disappointment at first.

Brother: Yes, I understand you experienced disappointment, but what did you find?

Coach: After trying several variations, I finally keyed in *"I steal"* and received back, *"Je vole"* which sounds just like *"Jubela."*

Brother: That's mind boggling!

Coach: I agree.

Brother: What did you do?

Coach: I started keying in more variations.

Brother: Did you eventually find others that fit?

Coach: No, and dismally so!

Brother: What was your next course of action?

Coach: In my frustration, I eventually used a voice to text translator and spoke into it every pronunciation of the first ruffian's name I could imagine.

Brother: And the translator gave you back the French equivalent of the English words you spoke?

Coach: It did, but nothing substantial. I finally tried something very simple. I said, *"jubel."*

Brother: What did it give you back?

Coach: Something amazing!

Brother: Do tell!

Coach: It gave me back the English *"I want."*

Brother: What did you do next?

Coach: I said *"I want"* in English and had it translate into French!

Brother: Interesting. What came back?

Coach: *"Je veux."*

Brother: *Je veux?*

Coach: Yes, and when I had the program read it back to me, I was amazed! It sounded almost like a slurred *"juh boo."*

Brother: Wait!? Are you saying the base of the ruffian names does actually come from French?

Coach: Yes I am. And the beginning two syllables are actually badly written words that all mean, *"I want"* in a form of French.

Brother: WOW! Then what do the ruffian names mean?

Coach: I'm getting to that. *"Jubela"* is the word I thought the professor shared in his video. It's what he claimed the child said.

Brother: Okay.

Coach: The professor wasn't truly correct in his assessment of what it meant, but he was close in that the child was telling him that he wanted something.

Brother: Did you figure it out?

Coach: Yes. When I put this phrase into the translator it gave me back, *"I want it."*

Brother: Are you saying the first ruffian's name means *"I want it."*

Coach: Yes. I am certainly saying just that! However, what I am also saying is that the words that have been characterized within ritual as names are not names at all!

Brother: I can see that! How does *"I want it"* appear as French?

Coach: *"Je veux le."* It is non standard French, but very understandable to someone speaking colloquial French such as the Joual dialect.

Brother: Awesome! What does the second ruffian's name mean?

Coach: I had very little success figuring it out at first. However, I had instant success with the third ruffian's name.

Brother: Okay. What does the third name mean?

Coach: It means *"I want light."*

Brother: How does that appear as French?

Coach: *"Je veux lum."*[19] I think that you'll agree that it sounds very much like *"Jubelum."*

Brother: Yes. And it makes a lot of sense!

Coach: How so?

Brother: These ruffian names, much like ritual in general, were never supposed to be written down and any words written would likely be phonetic renderings due to no English words matching these sounds.

Coach: Agreed!

Brother: What about the second name? Did you ever have any success figuring it out?

Coach: Yes, as my initial confidence might have alluded to. It took some doing and there were a lot of French words that could have been applied.

Brother: Like?

Coach: *"Leau"*, *"loos"*, and *"lowe"* were looked at very closely.

Brother: What do each mean within context?

Coach: *"Leau"* means *"water"*, *"Loos"* means *"advice; reward; reputation." "Lowe"* means *"to retain; to hire."*

Brother: Interesting! Are they all pronounced *"lo."*

Coach: Yes; or close enough for someone who doesn't speak French to assume there are no differences.

Brother: So which one is it? I want water? I want advice? I want reward? I want reputation? I want to be retained? I want to be hired? Please! I want to know!

Coach: As much as I wanted to lean toward *"loos"* because it fit with what I thought a ruffian might say, I had to go back to the basics of the Hiram Abiff story.

Brother: What did you find?

Coach: Well, I can see where one ruffian would say *"I want it."* And I can see where another ruffian would say *"I want light."* But nowhere did anyone say the obvious.

Brother: What do you mean?

Coach: Tell me please. What did each truly want?

Brother: They wanted to travel and earn wages as masters, without any liability or accountability.

Coach: Yes. And what one thing did they think they needed to do just that?

Brother: That's easy! They thought they needed the master's word... wait! That's it!

Coach: Yes?

Brother: They wanted *"The Masters Word!"*

Coach: They sure enough did!

Brother: Okay. I get it. They wanted *"The Word."*

Coach: Agreed!

Brother: So, how is *"I want the word"* said in French?

Coach: *"Je veux l'mot."* However, when the full phrase *"je veux le mot"* is translated back into English, it sometimes gives you a more colloquial *"I want to see it."*

Brother: Interesting. With the *"m"* being hardly heard and the *"t"* being silent, both sound almost like *"jubelo!"*

Coach: Yes!

Brother: So the second ruffian's name could be French for *"I want the word"* or, less formally, *"I want to see it?"*

Coach: Yes.

Brother: Wait! This is only first sinking in. The ruffians' names are actually sentences putting forth what each wants?

Coach: Yes. They are.

Brother: All that they are saying is literally, *"I want it! I want the word! I want light!"* or more figuratively *"I want it! I want to see it! I want light!"*

Coach: Yes. That's exactly what they are saying.

Brother: Okay. This raises a question.

Coach: Yes, at least one I can see immediately. What is that question?

Brother: How did these statements ever get twisted into our ritual as names?

Coach: That was a head stretcher for me as well. I had to look at the date of their first appearance for it to begin to make any sense.

Brother: You said it was 1760... What's so significant about that date?

Coach: It's after about twenty years of French exposures and influences upon English Freemasonic Ritual.

Brother: How does that fit in?

Coach: Joual is a French dialect used in Quebec that came over from northern France and is predominately old French[20] in origin. It became isolated from modern French development about 1760.

Brother: Isn't northern France right across the English Channel from London?

Coach: It certainly is. That's why this specific isolated dialect is extremely important to understand.

Brother: How's that?

Coach: British lodges had at least twenty years of constant exposure to northern French innovations to French ritual, all spoken in a Joual like dialect.

Brother: And?

Coach: The English speaking freemasons who saw these rituals eventually started writing about what they saw and heard.

Brother: So what you are implying is that English speaking freemasons saw and heard the Joual like dialect of the French freemasons acting out these three ruffians parts within their rituals, making demands and telling Hiram Abiff what they wanted from him, doing so in Joual, and the Englishmen merely wrote down what they thought they heard?

Coach: Exactly! And what do you think they heard each time.

Brother: Oh that's easy. *Jubela! Jubelo! Jubelum!*

Coach: Exactly! That's what I believe. How about you?

Brother: It makes perfect sense.

Coach: How so?

Brother: Well, for one, the names were written down based upon what the writer thought he heard.

Coach: What's more?

Brother: To compound matters, if he didn't understand French, especially this dialect, then he would not likely have any clue that these were not names at all!

Coach: I agree! What's further?

Brother: He applied in writing a phonetic rendering of what he thought he heard.

Coach: Meaning?

Brother: What he wrote was not written down in French; it was written down phonetically in English and to the best of the writer's ability.

Coach: And?

Brother: The author wrote these words down to the best of his abilities and referred to them as the ruffian's names. Everyone, especially Light seeking members, who tried to research these names thereafter, was likely tainted by this *"name"* assumption.

Coach: I can see that occurring.

Brother: Me too! Each researcher tried to make sense of these names as if what were shared actually were names and not the expressed desires of the ruffian characters!

Coach: What's more?

Brother: Because the dialect of northern France evolved quickly soon after 1760, even the French Freemasons who got a hold of English rituals thereafter would not be able to recognize the meanings behind the English rendered names.

Coach: So then, what do you know now about the meaning of the ruffian's names?

Brother: The first thing I know now is that they are not names at all!

Coach: And?

Brother: And that they were actually expressed desires.

Coach: What's more?

Brother: And the meaning behind each desire is what we all should be working toward as men and masons.

Coach: You haven't yet dealt with the other possibility!

Brother: What other possibility?

Coach: The possibility that those who were responsible for writing these ruffian names down, did so fully aware that the names were phonetic French renderings of the very things these ruffians were expressing to candidates who wanted what the ruffians desired and who didn't do the work required to obtain any of it.

Brother: Ah! So, it is a hidden message to be discovered by future generations?

Coach: It sure seems that way.

Brother: I'm seeing one thing more.

Coach: What's that?

Brother: It's far more an indirect warning to those who think that going through a degree is all that is required to obtain mastery.

Coach: Agreed! However, you forgot to ask me the obvious?

Brother: What's that?

Coach: What occurs when the French word *"want"* is substituted with the French word for *"steal?"*

Brother: Okay. Coach! What occurs when the word *"steal"* is used in place of *"want"* within these ruffian demands?

Coach: You get *"I steal it! I steal the word! I steal light!"* or more figuratively *"I steal it! I steal to see it! I steal light!"*

Brother: What words are used when these are communicated in French?

Coach: *Je vole le. Je vole l'mot. Je vole lum.* These statements are also somewhat close to the ruffian names.

Brother: How do we know whether *"want"* or *"steal"* is correct?

Coach: We don't. However, common sense says it is *"want"* and not *"steal."*

Brother: How did you arrive at your conclusion?

Coach: The ruffians demanded what they wanted from Hiram and in their own minds they had no intention of stealing anything.

Brother: Agreed. In their minds they were entitled to what they asked for, even though they truly didn't earn it.

Coach: Hence the logical conclusion is that they demanded what they wanted rather than what we as observers would conclude.

Brother: What's that?

Coach: That they didn't earn what they demanded and hence were in truth making efforts to steal.

Brother: They certainly were!

17. Raising Lessons

If the axe is dull and he does not sharpen its edge, then he must exert more strength. Wisdom has the advantage of giving success.
– Ecclesiastes 10:10

A Brother Asks: Coach, a question occurred to me, last night during School of Instruction, which I had not previously considered. I have not ever heard or read it being discussed. But it's more philosophical, I think, than ritual related. So, I'm considering it now.

Coach: Great! What is it?

Brother: Okay. King Solomon stands at the head of Hiram's grave and orders King Hiram to descend into the grave and raise Hiram Abiff's body.

Coach: Okay?

Brother: King Hiram fails at his efforts.

Coach: And?

Brother: Then instead of commanding him to descent into the grave a third time, Solomon says that he will descent into the grave and Raise the body in a specific manner.

Coach: Yes.

Brother: Here's the question that comes up for me when I think this through. Did Solomon assume that the King Hiram could not do what Solomon said he was going to do?

Coach: No.

Brother: Is it that some Masons are more skilled than others?

Coach: Not as related to the characters within this allegory.

Brother: Was it that King Solomon had some controlling tendencies?

Coach: No.

Brother: Then what lesson can be found here?

Coach: Do you want the lesson straight away or do you want to be guided through it?

Brother: Guidance always please!

Coach: Okay! Let's go through it together. What do the three Grand Masters represent?

Brother: Wisdom, Strength & Beauty.

Coach: Which of the three was assaulted, battered, murdered and buried?

Brother: Beauty.

Coach: Which of the three attempted to raise Beauty?

Brother: Strength of course.

Coach: So, what you are saying is that, according to the story as it is related to us, no matter how hard you try to bring forth Beauty, Strength is not enough?

Brother: I get that. But I also think of the two kings involved as being ascendant and equal.

Coach: The Characters they depict are equal in *"rank"* and they both were high in their respective standings. However, we are not talking about *"people"* here. This is an *"allegory"* and hence all people or things within the allegory are merely masks for ideals, concepts and principles.

Brother: Yes, this is true. I was viewing this from the point of view that the lesson is that equals have different strengths hence all Master Masons are not equal.

Coach: As in, each has different qualities, as in, *"characteristics"*, that each can draw upon as their strengths?

Brother: Yes, that's how I meant strengths in that statement.

Coach: Okay. Let's go down a side path. What is Strength?

Brother: Strength is power... brute force!

Coach: I propose to you that Strength is not power. Power is flowing potential. Strength is that potential but it is not flowing. In other words, Strength is *"Inventory"* or *"Resources."* Think this through, what was King Hiram to King Solomon?

Brother: Ah! Yes! I get it! King Hiram was King Solomon's resource guy.

Coach: How do you know this?

Brother: Well, from the Lecture and also from scripture.

Coach: Yes, that's what I found! So, let's go back to the story. King Hiram was the resource guy and he represented what?

Brother: Strength. And that comes directly from the fact that he had inventory to offer.

Coach: And Hiram Abiff, what did he represent?

Brother: Beauty.

Coach: Did King Hiram succeed in raising Beauty?

Brother: No.

Coach: So Strength alone could not do it?

Brother: That's my understanding. But let me take it from here.

Coach: Go for it!

Brother: Wisdom could!

Coach: And what is all this trying to say to the candidate?

Brother: That no matter what resources, or strengths, you may think you possess, Strength alone cannot raise Beauty.

Coach: Yes! Spot on.

Brother: Thanks! Let me expand upon this theme.

Coach: Go ahead.

Brother: It's letting me know that no matter

what resources I may think I have to complete a task, these alone cannot bring forth Beauty in what I'm attempting to accomplish.

Coach: Agreed! Let's continue on the Strength topic... What is *"Light?"*

Brother: Sometimes it's just information. Other times, it's Knowledge.

Coach: Is it ever Wisdom?

Brother: No.

Coach: Why Not?

Brother: Because you can only share your knowledge. You cannot share your wisdom.

Coach: Why Not?

Brother: Because wisdom is a skill, and you cannot give a skill to another person.

Coach: I agree. But let's take a look at this more closely. Why not?

Brother: Because Wisdom has to do with personal development and no one can develop personal skills for anyone else.

Coach: So, no matter how many Resources (Strengths) you might receive from someone else, you must still develop Wisdom for yourself?

Brother: Yes!

Coach: Agreed. Let's get back to your questions and recap. Once again, what was required to bring forth Beauty?

Brother: Wisdom... but that only comes with time and observation.

Coach: You mean, *"skill development"* backed by experience?

Brother: Yes! However, in the Allegory, and from my perspective, Wisdom was frustrated as well and required Strength.

Coach: You're saying that no action Solomon directed his Resources to take for him gave him the results he wanted? He must have been extremely frustrated!

Brother: Exactly!

Coach: When he realized this, what did Wisdom then ask of Strength?

Brother: Essentially, in this our present condition, what shall we do?

Coach: Please clarify your point.

Brother: Strength had to guide Wisdom to the obvious.

Coach: Yes, and what did Wisdom do just prior to his effort?

Brother: Set the expectation?

Coach: Sure. Take a knee with me for a moment and think this through a bit deeper.

Brother: Like, take a breath, purge the emotion, and think logically before acting?

Coach: That usually helps, but it is not the direction to which I was alluding.

Brother: What direction was that?

Coach: Brother, what does *"take a knee"* mean to you?

Brother: Okay. I get it. You are referring to prayer, just as within ritual. Wisdom and Strength were asking for God to step in, or intervene.

Coach: Yes. More specifically, Wisdom was asking for guidance from Strength. He then received the suggestion of prayer from his trusted Resource guy.

Brother: But, in the end that too was not successful because Beauty was not Raised.

Coach: How so?

Brother: Why else would the two kings take him up as close to the temple as Jewish laws of that day allowed and then bury him again?

Coach: Once again you are doing what many do when it comes to Allegory.

Brother: What's that?

Coach: You're confusing the allegorical characters, Wisdom, Strength and Beauty, with what each character represents within the allegory, the two kings and the remaining bones of Hiram.

Brother: How's that?

Coach: There is the *"story"* focus and there are the concepts that the story focus is trying to convey.

Brother: Please explain this with a little more detail.

Coach: Sure. In the latter, the Allegorical part, the very core of Beauty was actually Raised. This was acted out by Hiram's bones being pulled up out of the grave. And it was not Strength that did this; it was Wisdom. In the story part it says the bones of Hiram Abiff were pulled out and properly buried elsewhere.

Brother: Okay.

Coach: The Allegory communicates Light, information and knowledge, which we must make effort to decode, using skills developed by experience.

Brother: This is beginning to make sense.

Coach: Good. Here's the kicker... Prayer is essential for any grand and important undertaking, including bringing forth beauty.

Brother: Agreed!

Coach: Do you remember when this concept was first put forth to you?

Brother: Yes.

Coach: When?

Brother: At the very beginning of my first Degree.

Coach: Do you see the technique being used here?

Brother: Yes.

Coach: What is it?

Brother: Inculcation. Ritual keeps coming back to one of the very first things conveyed upon my Entry into the Craft.

Coach: Yes it does do this.

Brother: Let me try to put this all together. The purpose of the processional was to assist King Solomon (Wisdom) in Raising Hiram's body (Beauty). King Hiram (Strength) tried to help but, at one point, King Solomon had a moment of panic and called upon Strength for different help. Strength helps by telling Wisdom to pray. It was prayer that provided the path to Raising Beauty.

Coach: Why do you say Wisdom had a moment of panic?

Brother: Wisdom's use of the grand hailing sign was followed by asking Strength for guidance.

Coach: Please recall the words that were used when he used that sign.

Brother: Done.

Coach: Was that a moment of panic or was it a moment of despair?

Brother: Ok, despair does fit the scene better, especially with the words he used. Wisdom needed guidance from Strength to know how to proceed because he lost hope in the moment.

Coach: Yes. What you're saying is that Wisdom, not knowing what to do, made effort to retrieve further resources (options) and what came back from Strength (Inventory) was what Resource?

Brother: The *"prayer"* option! Let us pray.

Coach: Yes. This sounds like an excellent option.

Brother: I translate that to *"We need divine help here."*

Coach: Especially when there was no hope, as in, *"despair denies the existence of hope."*[21]

Brother: Yes. That makes perfect sense as long as we don't follow the story line from there in the degree ritual and the lecture.

Coach: How so?

Brother: Well the parts about re-burial and also incineration.

Coach: Of course. That is where the story and the Allegory split, and for good reason too.

Brother: How's that?

Coach: Having the main message communicated at the point of the Raising, the story goes on to its logical conclusion, unless you're a freemasonic resurrection conspiracy theorist, then all bets are off.

Brother: So true!

Coach: But the lesson is communicated quite clearly to those who have done the Apprentice and Fellow Craft Work.

Brother: What's that?

Coach: Those that have not done the Work have gotten buried in the Rubbish along with the Beauty, for they do not have Wisdom's Passport, which is an entirely different rabbit's hole.

Brother: Yet, did not Wisdom eventually use Strength to raise Beauty?

Coach: Are you asking if Wisdom used his own Strength or if Wisdom used Strength in the form of the Strong Grip of the Lion's Paw of Judea?

Brother: If it is taken as story, then King Solomon used his own strength in the form of the strong grip of the lion's paw of Judah.

Coach: And if it is taken as allegory?

Brother: If it is taken as allegory, then Wisdom requires the use of this same grip to bring forth Beauty from the grave.

Coach: Agreed. So, let's get back to your original question.

Brother: Which was?

Coach: What lesson can be found here?

Brother: Ah! Understand that allegory has both a story level that can be misleading and an underlying level that communicates messages only when the seeker takes time to perpend them thoroughly.

Coach: Agreed!

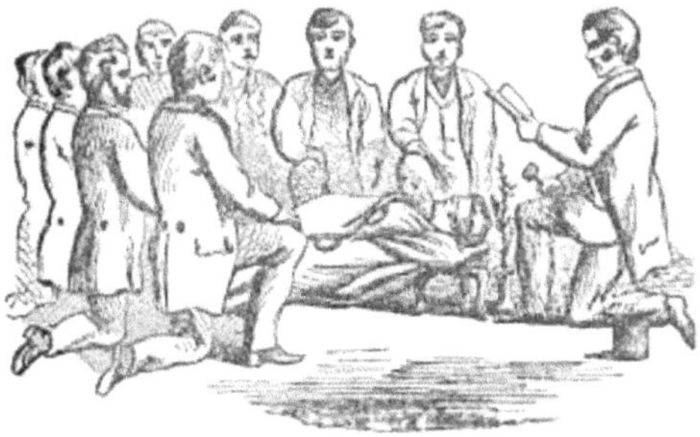

18. The Grasp

This is the reason that I speak to them in parables: because having the power of seeing, they do not see; and having the power of hearing, they do not hear, nor do they grasp and understand. – Matthew 13:13

Brother: Why is the Lion's Paw of Judah used to Raise Hiram?

Coach: Before we get into it, what can you tell me about this specific grasp?

Brother: It's not a particularly functional configuration.

Coach: Are you implying that the mechanics of the actual grip could be better for grasping?

Brother: Yes. I am implying this, and you do speak to what I have observed.

Coach: If the actual grip is not as functional as if could be for grasping, what might this imply?

Brother: That it is not the actual grip that is important.

Coach: That's my take, except for perhaps performing ritual. What would be important about the grip?

Brother: I sense it is the message behind the name of the grip.

Coach: What can you tell me about the name?

Brother: It refers to Judah.

Coach: Who was Judah?

Brother: Judah was son of Jacob and Leah. It was his father, Jacob, who first referred to his son as a *"young lion."* This reference was put forth in the Jewish naming custom that provides a substitute for a person's true name which sometimes becomes paired in usage.

Coach: How was he eventually referred to as a result of his father's reference?

Brother: The lion of the tribe of Judah.

Coach: What other historical figures were also referred to by this phrase?

Brother: Those individuals who claim his bloodline.

Coach: Can you provide some examples?

Brother: Yes, King Solomon, Jesus the Nazarene and rulers of Ethiopia up until 1974.

Coach: What is significant about this title?

Brother: Allegorically, it denotes both courage and sovereignty.

Coach: And the grasp?

Brother: It is one that embodies a grasp that is lionesque, as in, one that is courageous, authoritative and self-governing.

Coach: How does it differ from other grips used within the Craft?

Brother: The very lowest grip is superficial. It only grasps things that appear upon the surface and nothing that is covered or concealed.

Coach: What about the grip that is one step beyond this one?

Brother: That grip does get below the surface and does grasp things that are concealed and not revealed by superficial examination.

Coach: What's missing?

Brother: It doesn't grasp the very core of what is being handled.

Coach: What of the highest grip, the one referred to as the lion's paw?

Brother: It grasps well-beyond the surface, past the mechanics and into the very core of what is required to fully comprehend what is being dealt with.

Coach: How does this grip embody courage, authority and self-government?

Brother: A person with this grasp is compelled to face things, people, and situations regardless of possible dangers.

Coach: What else?

Brother: A person with this grasp comes from a place of authority.

Coach: What does this mean?

Brother: The individual has the necessary resources, suitable experiences and honed skills that make this grip power filled.

Coach: What's more?

Brother: A person who has this grasp has laid the foundation required to suitably and proficiently govern himself.

Coach: Why is this so important?

Brother: Without self-discipline, all other disciplines are practiced without a strong foundation of support.

Coach: So, let's get back to your original question, *"Why is the Lion's Paw of Judah used to Raise Hiram?"*

Brother: Okay. The first aspect that needs to be noted is that it is not superficial.

Coach: Agreed!

Brother: And it goes far beyond the simple mechanics that lay below the surface.

Coach: Yes, and?

Brother: It appears to exemplify someone who grasps the very core of what is before him, and does so willingly facing potential dangers with necessary resources, suitable experiences, and honed skills that come from mature self-governing disciplines.

Coach: Was all that required from Wisdom to bring forth Beauty?

Brother: Yes. It certainly was!

Coach: What does this imply?

Brother: You cannot rely upon wisdom that is second hand?

Coach: Second hand?

Brother: Yes. If you are told something that is wise, then it is merely inventory and not wisdom itself.

Coach: How so?

Brother: Knowledge is inventory. It takes wisdom to apply this inventory appropriately.

Coach: Give me more details please.

Brother: That application cannot be done without suitable experience, honed skills and personal discipline to govern that application.

Coach: Ah! So, wisdom cannot be inventory then?

Brother: It cannot.

Coach: Why?

Brother: Although wisdom draws from inventories of experience, skills and disciplines, it is the masterful application of these three that produces that which is wise.

Coach: Is this why lesser grasps do not bring forth masterful results?

Brother: Yes!

ᒪ⊓⌐ ⊐ᒪ ∨ᒧ>⊐⊐∨ <□∨⊐ ⌐ᒪᒧ⊏ ᒧ>∨⊐⊓⌐□∨∧;
⌐>□∨ᒪ >⊐⊏□⊏ᒪ ∨⊐ᒪ□⌐ ∨ᒪᒧ⊔⊐ᒪ⌐∨ ⊓ᒪ
⌐ᒪ⊏□⊐□⊓>∨ ⊏ᒧ<. – ⊐ᒧ⌐⊏ ⊐ᒧ□

19. Resurrecting Hiram

By the sweat of your face you will eat bread, Till you return to the ground, Because from it you were taken; For you are dust, And to dust you shall return." – Genesis 3:19

A Brother Asks: Coach, was Hiram Abiff Resurrected?

Coach: Why do you ask?

Brother: Because I'm getting a lot of conflicting responses from Brothers within my lodge. And I have to say that the responses to my question are all over the place. It's very frustrating.

Coach: The answer is *"No."*

Brother: No?

Coach: *"No"* it is.

Brother: That's it?

Coach: Yes!

Brother: What about all the members who look at the entire third degree drama through religious eyes.

Coach: What about them?

Brother: Many of them claim, and do so quite forcefully, that Hiram was resurrected.

Coach: What they claim is unsupported by the story. They are mistaken.

Brother: But they say that each Candidate is raised from the grave, and he is alive.

Coach: Well of course he is. He was never dead to begin with. He is playing the part of a corpse, but the candidate is not a corpse, is he?

Brother: Well no, not really.

Coach: Of course he isn't. You can't well have a dead candidate playing the role of a corpse can you? It's simply counterproductive to bringing in new members.

Brother: That's not what I mean.

Coach: What *do* you mean?

Brother: Well, he's raised and he's alive. Doesn't that make him resurrected?

Coach: Who's raised and who's alive?

Brother: Well, Hiram is raised, and it's clear that he is alive.

Coach: You're mixing up the candidate portraying a role within ritual with the character that he is playing.

Brother: Huh?

Coach: The Candidate is *"playing"* the part of Hiram and the candidate is surely alive. However, at the end of the story, the man the candidate is portraying, Hiram, is not alive.

Brother: I follow you on this. But I've played the part of Hiram. It's clear to me that I was raised and someone talked with me when I was.

Coach: Yes and that experience playing Hiram understandably confuses many members.

Brother: Then what are we not seeing?

Coach: Great Question! From the story it is quite clear that Hiram is dead. Furthermore, his skin and muscle were pulling away from his bones at the time of his body's discovery and attempted recovery. This tells us that he has been dead for some time.

Brother: Exactly! However, he was raised and the person who raised him talked with him!

Coach: What is occurring for you right now occurs for many others at this point.

Brother: What's that?

Coach: You're assuming that talking with the candidate at the point of the body's raising is akin to talking with Hiram. It's this action that creates your confusion. Herein lays your challenge.

Brother: What's that?

Coach: You think that the candidate *is* Hiram at the point of this talk.

Brother: Well, yes.

Coach: He is not.

Brother: What?

Coach: Think about it. The end of the story is the raising of a dead body. What follows that end of the story is for the candidate's benefit. The play continues, but in a different direction. There is a very fuzzy demarcation to the end of the story and it is purposeful.

Brother: It's all very confusing!

Coach: You are not alone in this confusion.

Brother: I'm not?

Coach: You're like many others who have experienced this allegorical play. Playing a part does not make you the character you're playing. The candidate was not Hiram. He was playing the *"part"* of Hiram. It was Hiram that died, not the actor playing the part of Hiram. It was the candidate who heard the words, not Hiram.

Brother: Can you explain it to me again please?

Coach: Sure! You've confused the player of the part being played with the character being played.

Brother: How so?

Coach: The play clearly states that the Grand Master's body was badly deteriorated by the time it was found.

Brother: So?

Coach: It was so badly decayed that all that the retrievers could grab a hold of and pull up from the grave were the bones.

Brother: Okay.

Coach: Moreover, his remains were taken out of the grave and properly buried thereafter. You do not bury a resurrected body and in truth, you would not want to be doing this to a live candidate either. You might get some objections.

Brother: But couldn't Hiram have been resurrected and then have died much later, thus requiring a proper interment of his body.

Coach: Sure. You can make up whatever you want about the story. However, you would have to add to the story to make what you claim supported.

Brother: Huh?

Coach: As the story exists, he was murdered, his body was buried, then disinterred, then reburied, then disinterred again in a highly degraded condition. His remains were then exhumed and then properly buried. The fact that you have a live body playing the part of a dead man at that moment has no relevance whatsoever to the story.

Brother: But can't it be interpreted that he was resurrected?

Coach: Sure it could. But the story simply does not support that.

Brother: How so?

Coach: Think about it!

Brother: I thought I had. What am I missing?

Coach: I'm glad you asked. Let me pose a question back to you. *What was the whole reason it was so important to find Hiram?*

Brother: So the three Grand Masters could come together once again to bring forth *"The Master's Word."*

Coach: Exactly!

Brother: What am I missing?

Coach: If Hiram was truly resurrected, wouldn't he be fully capable of rendering that Word with the other three cast members?

Brother: Well, sure. That makes sense.

Coach: Then what follows does not make sense.

Brother: What's that?

Coach: If Hiram was actually resurrected, there would be absolutely no reason for that other word.

Brother: How so?

Coach: Hiram would be alive and fully capable of continuing as he had done so before. Hence, the Master's Word would not have to be rediscovered by anyone into the future because we would still have it if Hiram were still alive.

Brother: There's one more thing to add here.

Coach: What's that?

Brother: The other word, the offered substitute, would serve no purpose whatsoever.

Coach: Agreed!

ΓLV>ΓΓLUV: VΠ ΓOVL ΠΓ ΓJOVL LΓΠ7
VƎL ШLJШ; VΠ ΓLVVΠΓL, JΓO7Ǝ ΠΓ JL
JΓΠ>ƎƎV JJUC VΠ COLL; VΠ JΓO7Ǝ
JJUC O7VΠ >VL ΠΓ JUVO>OVΛ; ΓL>O>L;
VΠ ΓL7L<

20. The Substitute

Wealth obtained by fraud will dwindle, but whoever earns it through labor will multiply it. – Proverbs 13:11

A Brother Asks: What does the Substitute word truly mean?

Coach: What were you told that it means?

Brother: I was informed by ritual that it was Hebrew for *"what the builder."*

Coach: Yes. You were. However, this is not true.

Brother: Why do you say this?

Coach: Because it is not Hebrew and any effort to prove that it is requires a forced and illogical explanation.

Brother: But why would I be told something that was not true?

Coach: Let me respond to your question by asking you one in return.

Brother: Okay.

Coach: Did you do both the Apprentice and Fellow Craft Work to which Rituals direct you?

Brother: I did the proficiencies that were required of me by my lodge Brothers.

Coach: Yes. I understand that you learned the answers to certain questions, and were given some words and grips to use appropriately.

Brother: Yes.

Coach: However, you did not answer my question.

Brother: I thought that I did.

Coach: Yes. I get that. However, let me break the question down into parts and ask you again.

Brother: Okay.

Coach: Did you learn to subdue your passions and keep your desires within due bounds?

Brother: Well, not yet. Isn't that ongoing though?

Coach: The refinement of the skills is ongoing.

Brother: Agreed!

Coach: However, the basic skills are something that you must learn in order to refine what you learned.

Brother: Interesting.

Coach: Hence the question. I shall reword it.

Brother: Okay.

Coach: Have you learned the basics yet?

Brother: Well, no. Not when you ask me like that.

Coach: Can I assume too that you have yet to learn how to manage your time?

Brother: Well, I'm working on that still.

Coach: How about setting priorities based upon what's important?

Brother: I'm not quite sure as to what is truly important yet, so I guess I would have to say, *"not yet"* to that also.

Coach: How about your vices and superfluities?

Brother: What about them?

Coach: Have you divested yourself of them yet?

Brother: That's impossible.

Coach: Why do you say this?

Brother: Well for one, no one is perfect!

Coach: How are you defining the word *"perfect?"*

Brother: Flawless.

Coach: What if I told you the word *"perfect"* as applied to Masonic efforts actually means *"mature"* and *"suitable for the builder's use?"*

Brother: That puts a different light on my effort.

Coach: How so?

Brother: It means that I would have to work toward making myself suitable and mature.

Coach: Yes, it does. So, do you actually know what your vices and superfluities are?

Brother: No. Not really.

Coach: Then tell me... How are you going to use your common gavel to divest yourself of them if you don't know what they are?

Brother: I guess I would have a difficult time doing this since I do not know what to divest.

Coach: Agreed! I'll stop asking about the apprentice Work since it is obvious you have yet to start it, much less complete it.

Brother: Thanks. I appreciate this. That line of questioning was making me feel uncomfortable.

Coach: Yes. I could tell. How about the Fellow Craft Work?

Brother: Like I said, I did that already.

Coach: So, you are proficient in Grammar, Logic and Rhetoric?

Brother: Well, no; not really. I've done a little reading and studying on those subjects. But I can't truly say that I am proficient in each.

Coach: How about Arithmetic, Geometry, Music and Astronomy?

Brother: I can do math and some geometry. Does playing music and looking through a telescope count for the other two?

Coach: What do you think?

Brother: I guess not from the way you're asking me this. What does any of this have to do with the substitute?

Coach: I'm glad you asked. Let me ask a few more questions and maybe our concerted effort will shed a little light on it for you.

Brother: Good. Fire away!

Coach: What did the ruffians want?

Brother: They wanted to be able to travel, work, and earn master's wages.

Coach: Yes! And what did they think they had to have to have that occur?

Brother: The secrets, and more specifically, *"The Master's Word."*

Coach: Yes! And did they earn the secrets, namely The Master's Word?

Brother: According to the story, they had not completed the Temple and hence did not earn the secrets. That's why they approached Master Hiram. They figured they could obtain it from him, with a little persuasion.

Coach: Yes. They did think this. Are you telling me they didn't complete the Work they committed themselves to do, and they wanted something they didn't earn?

Brother: Yes. I guess I am saying just that.

Coach: In your view and that of ritual, did they deserve the Master's Word?

Brother: No. They did not earn it.

Coach: I agree. Let me take this in a different direction. When you undertook the role of Hiram Abiff, what was it that you expected?

Brother: I expected to obtain the title of *"Master Mason"* and learn the secrets of a Master Mason.

Coach: And so you paid a fee and went through the ritual.

Brother: Yes! I did just that.

Coach: Did you get the title?

Brother: I sure did!

Coach: Did you get the secrets?

Brother: Well, I got a password, a grip and a substitute for The Master's Word.

Coach: Why do you think you got a substitute?

Brother: Because the Master's Word was lost.

Coach: And you believe that?

Brother: Why of course! Why shouldn't I?

Coach: Well for one, there are still master masons traveling, working and earning master's wages to this day. Doesn't that raise a question or two for you?

Brother: Well, that's because they have the substitute.

Coach: Haven't you thought this through?

Brother: Huh? I'm guessing by the way you fired that question at me so quickly that I haven't. I think I might be missing something here.

Coach: I agree with your assessment. What do you think it is that is missing?

Brother: Well, for one, the Master's Word. That's missing!

Coach: Is it?

Brother: That's what I am being told. But wait! That hasn't seemed to have prevented others from traveling, working and earning. I mean, after all, there have been some pretty awesome masterful works produced since Solomon's time.

Coach: I agree!

Brother: But I can't contribute all of that to them using a substitute.

Coach: Why's that?

Brother: Because the substitute alone will not produce masterful works.

Coach: Why do you say that?

Brother: Because the substitute is used only as a mode of recognition. It doesn't do anything else for the person who has or uses it.

Coach: Agreed! So what is it that these masters have that you still don't?

Brother: The ability to produce masterpieces and get paid for doing so?

Coach: So what is it that makes these substitute carrying travelers masterful enough to work and earn master's wages?

Brother: They must be in possession of secrets that allow them to do all these things.

Coach: So, it's the secrets that allow them to do this?

Brother: It must be this. What else could it be?

Coach: Could it be something that they received during the third degree ritual?

Brother: It's not likely.

Coach: Why?

Brother: Well, I went through the very same degree and I didn't receive anything that made me masterful. All I received were a title, some more words and grips.

Coach: So, you agree that you don't truly possess anything from the third degree that qualifies as making you masterful enough to travel, work and earn master's wages?

Brother: I guess I am saying just that in a roundabout way.

Coach: Then, in a roundabout way you are saying that you are not the real thing?

Brother: Real thing?

Coach: Yes, as in, you are not masterful, and that you stood in as a substitute for the masterful Hiram Abiff without being masterful yourself.

Brother: Ouch!

Coach: Why does this pain you so my Brother?

Brother: Because I just realized the substitute is me, and not that word I was given.

Coach: And?

Brother: I don't think I possess the skills of a master.

Coach: And?

Brother: It is no small wonder that I was handed a substitute rather than the real thing.

Coach: What can you do about it?

Brother: I guess I should go back to square one and actually earn the title I currently wear.

Coach: That would be a great start. What's the lesson presented here?

Brother: Until I actually develop myself and do so masterfully, I only provide a substitute to others and myself.

Coach: A valuable lesson to walk away with?

Brother: Yes! And it will only be valuable when I do something with it.

Coach: Agreed!

21. The Master's Word

And every man who strives for mastery exercises self-control in all things. Indeed therefore those men do it so that they might obtain a perishable crown, but we do so to obtain an imperishable one. – 1 Cor. 9:25

A Brother Asks: What can you tell me about the Master's Word?

Coach: What would you like to know?

Brother: Well for one, why does everyone want it?

Coach: Ritual tells us that possession of it allows for some empowering benefits. There are a lot of people who want them.

Brother: What are these benefits?

Coach: To travel to foreign countries, to work, to earn master's wages, to support and to contribute.

Brother: Those are pretty powerful incentives!

Coach: They certainly are.

Brother: What is it about the Master's Word that allows for all these benefits to occur?

Coach: Great question! What is it that you think this Word offers to those who have it?

Brother: Well, in the case of travel, I think it might work as some sort of passport that allows passage.

Coach: You mean like revealing it to those who might block your path so that they will let you through?

Brother: Yes. Exactly!

Coach: How does the bearer reveal it while traveling?

Brother: I guess he would simply reveal it, others would recognize it and they would then let the revealer continue.

Coach: Isn't there some sort of restrictions on how the word can be revealed?

Brother: Yes. The Word can only be revealed in the presence and agreement of the three Grand Masters.

Coach: Sounds like you're going to have some traveling companions with you should you want to reveal the Word so that you can Travel.

Brother: I had not thought that my traveling requiring partners.

Coach: Let's say that's not a problem. How about revealing the Word while you work?

Brother: Okay, I can see where this is going. How am I going to Work and Earn Master's Wages by revealing the Word if I don't have the three Grand Masters there to reveal it?

Coach: My thoughts exactly!

Brother: Wow! This does present a bit of a challenge.

Coach: It certainly does!

Brother: Do you think the ruffians thought this through?

Coach: Not for one moment.

Brother: I don't think this line of thinking is what was intended.

Coach: How so?

Brother: Well, the assumptions about the Word that were made by the ruffians simply don't bring about a Word that is useful.

Coach: I agree!

Brother: And as a result, many Brothers pursuing the Word assume the very same thing that the ruffians assume.

Coach: What's that?

Brother: That the Word is something that can be handed over from one person to the next.

Coach: Is it something that can be handed over from one person to another?

Brother: It doesn't seem like it is.

Coach: Then what might it be?

Brother: That's something that I am pursuing through this conversation.

Coach: Good!

Brother: I guess I have to look at the parameters more closely.

Coach: That would be a great start.

Brother: What is it that a man can carry with him, which would allow him to travel, work, and earn masterfully?

Coach: Great question! Add to this that he must be able to do all this by himself with no help from others.

Brother: Interesting addition. I can see that this constraint should apply.

Coach: Why?

Brother: Because a Master should not require outside assistance to render masterpieces.

Coach: Masterpieces?

Brother: Yes. Masterpieces! If you are going to be viewed to be a master, you must be masterful in what you do such that what you render are masterpieces.

Coach: But to reveal the Word, don't you have to have the presence and agreement of the three.

Brother: Yes. This presents a paradox.

Coach: What's that?

Brother: Masters should be able to do all this alone. Yet to do this masterfully, one must reveal the Word. Yet to reveal the Word, the presence and agreement of the three must occur. My head is spinning!

Coach: There truly is no paradox.

Brother: Yet I just put one forth.

Coach: You did appear to. And if you examine the paradox closely, you'll likely see that it is the way that you are viewing the information that creates the paradox.

Brother: Can you walk me through it?

Coach: Of course. Let's examine the premises.

Brother: Okay.

Coach: One of the premises is that the three must be present and in agreement for the Word to be revealed.

Brother: Yes. That refers to the three Grand Masters.

Coach: Yes. But what actually must be present and in agreement?

Brother: You said *"what"* and not *"who."* Are you hinting at something?

Coach: I am.

Brother: *What* must be present and in agreement *rather than who?* I guess I have to go back and look at this as allegory.

Coach: Yes. That is correct. Let's both do this.

Brother: Well, we are told that the three Grand Masters represent things.

Coach: They truly do. What do they represent?

Brother: They represent Wisdom, Strength and Beauty.

Coach: Agreed!

Brother: Are you saying that the three that are present and in agreement are Wisdom, Strength and Beauty?

Coach: I'm not. But I know that the allegory is clearly saying this.

Brother: Wow! So, to reveal the Word, Wisdom, Strength and Beauty must be present and in agreement?

Coach: Are you asking or telling me?

Brother: Yes. I mean no. I mean...yes I am telling you and no I am no longer asking.

Coach: What are you saying?

Brother: I was taking this story as literal and not allegorical. I'm not doing that any more.

Coach: Good! What have you concluded?

Brother: The Master's Word is a metaphor!

Coach: It truly is. For what is it a metaphor?

Brother: It would have to be skill and moral development.

Coach: Why would it have to be this?

Brother: Because a person's skills and morality are the only things that would enable travel, work and earning at a master's level.

Coach: How so?

Brother: If the person did not have a master's skills and morality, travel, work and earning would not occur at a master's level.

Coach: And what are the qualities that make a person's skills and morality masterful?

Brother: That would be the presence and agreement of the three.

Coach: And they are?

Brother: Wisdom, Strength and Beauty!

Coach: So what is the Lost Word?

Brother: It is any person who has not taken the time to develop and hone skills and morals where Wisdom, Strength and Beauty are present and in agreement.

Coach: Yes! How does the Word allow a person to travel, work and earn master's wages?

Brother: All those people with integrity who are able to recognize and pay for mastery will do so willingly and without hesitation.

Coach: Why?

Brother: Because they know they are going to receive that for which they pay.

Coach: And those who are not masterful?

Brother: They will be seen for who they truly are and be paid accordingly.

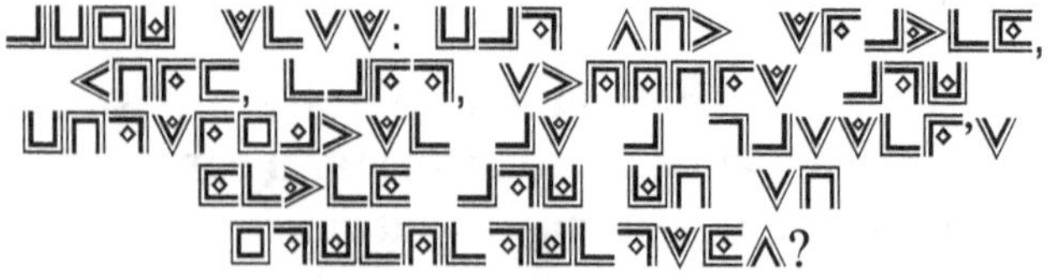

22. Where the Masters Are

And they gave it to the overseers of the work of the Lord's house, and the overseers gave it to the workmen working in the house, for building it up and making good what was damaged;
– 2 Chronicles 34:10

A Brother Asks: I understand the Freemasonic Roadmaps, the Work they point toward, and the conceptual ideas behind each of them. However, I have yet to meet one of these perfect and Masterful men.

Coach: This saddens me to hear this Brother.

Brother: Just how do you find one? Ask the Dali llama? Most Grand Masters I've met aren't overly masterful either. Is there a secret list of them in some dusty archive somewhere? Coach, help me out here!

Coach: They are out there my Brother! I have seen them. I have talked with them. I have become friends with them. And I have learned from them.

Brother: Let me ask you differently then. How do I find them still?

Coach: I look for evidence. Masterpieces are a dead giveaway.

Brother: I understand. Masters make masterpieces because they are masterful.

Coach: I also don't sabotage my efforts by defining the word *"perfect"* to be *"flawless"* when I seek them.

Brother: How do you define the word when you are seeking a master?

Coach: Maturity. I look for it in masters. It more suitably reflects what I seek and it is upon this attribute that my eyes continually focus.

Brother: That makes sense. It also makes it easier for me to identify a master.

Coach: How's that?

Brother: Immaturity is very easy to spot and maturity tends to stand out in a crowd of immature people.

Coach: I agree. I also look for Work being done, and done better than it was done the previous day.

Brother: Ah! So Masters continually perfect what they do.

Coach: Yes. They practice daily an honorable and consistent stewardship over their tools and skills.

Brother: Like keeping their tools and skills sharp and true?

Coach: Yes, exactly that.

Brother: Are there any other things that you look for?

Coach: Yes. I also look for the well-written Roadmaps that they have created and left for their fellow travelers to follow so that those travelers can also develop and cultivate Mastery in themselves. Those maps certainly make it easier to identify the Work to be done, should these travelers and others choose to do it.

Brother: Okay, I had not thought about that before.

Coach: When you do, what occurs for you?

Brother: I remember the times I have picked up books written by people whose works I admired.

Coach: I have had that realization many times. The classics are all written by masters.

Brother: What else do you look for?

Coach: I apply the Master's Word Acid Test.

Brother: The acid test?

Coach: Yes. I seek only those who have combined measures of Wisdom, Strength & Beauty in such a way that they are all present and all in agreement.

Brother: I had not thought of doing that either.

Coach: I did not do that at first, but after dealing with a few false masters, I learned to look for specific signs, words and points. The acid test is just one of a few.

Brother: I find myself filled with despair. I don't think I shall ever find a master based upon what you have shared.

Coach: Please, don't lose heart. They are out there my Brother.

Brother: But where?

Coach: They are not easy to find. Especially by those who are hoodwinked by Craft dogma, laziness and misinformation designed to keep members chained to the walls of ignorance, naiveté and doubt.

Brother: Are you telling me there are members of the craft that do not want others to be aware that there are masters among us?

Coach: Yes. However, you can spot these ruffians and cowans fairly easily. But let's not get off topic.

Brother: Agreed. We have already covered that.

Coach: Yes, we have. But let me steer this in a different direction.

Brother: Okay.

Coach: I was given something the other day. I was aware of it before, but the reminder is timely for it to be included in this conversation.

Brother: What was that?

Coach: I was given the biblical description of the classes of worker at King Solomon's temple.

Brother: What were they?

Coach: They were the Laborers, who were the Apprentices.

Brother: Yes. We have them in the Craft as well.

Coach: Yes. Above them in class were the Skilled Workers, who were the Fellows of the Craft. Above the Fellow Craft in skill were the Overseers or Masters of the Craft.

Brother: That fits nicely with what we have within our Blue Lodge.

Coach: Yes. I think in light of your question, I have a passage to share with you as a great resource to review and to be included as an insightful tool in your quest to find Masterful men.

Brother: Please do share.

Coach: I label this *"Qualifications of Overseers"* and it goes like this...

> *This is a faithful saying: If a man desires the position of a bishop,*[22] *he desires a good work. A bishop then must be blameless, the husband of one wife, temperate, sober-minded, of good behavior, hospitable, able to teach; not given to wine, not violent, not greedy for money, but gentle, not quarrelsome, not covetous; one who rules*

his own house well, having his children in submission with all reverence (for if a man does not know how to rule his own house, how will he take care of the church of God?); not a novice, lest being puffed up with pride he fall into the same condemnation as the devil. Moreover he must have a good testimony among those who are outside, lest he fall into reproach and the snare of the devil.

Brother: That sounds like scripture. Where does it come from?

Coach: This quote came from the Volume of Sacred Law, 1 Timothy 3. I do believe it speaks well to some of what you are seeking and is a good information base to create a starter list for yourself.

Brother: It does just that.

Coach: One last comment. First, be what you seek. I hope you get the message that I imply.

Brother: Yes. I do get the message and it is startlingly clear.

Coach: Good. Someday I hope you'll recognize the master you seek when you see your masterful Works reflected back to you.

Brother: I look forward to that day.

23. What Was Lost

I will seek that which was lost and bring back that which has strayed, and I will bandage the hurt and the crippled and will strengthen the weak and the sick, but I will destroy the fat and the strong who have become hardhearted and perverse; I will feed them with judgment and punishment.– Ezekiel 34:16

A Brother Asks: What was Lost with the Grand Master's Death?

Coach: All that he did to develop and employ his masterful abilities and grant access to the same through him.

Brother: Would you expand upon this further.

Coach: Sure. The Master's Word is a composite of Beauty, Strength and Wisdom, of which manifest the Masterful Artisan-Teacher.[23]

Brother: Can you break it down further for me?

Coach: I sure can. Beauty, if we go by what some rituals imply, is the result-filled application of Cunning Craftsmanship which is utterly impossible without Wisdom to Contrive and Resources with which to Build.

Brother: Wait! Cunning Craftsmanship?

Coach: Yes, as in the original sense of the word.

Brother: What's the original sense?

Coach: The original sense was *"possessing erudition or skill"* and it had no implications of deceit at all.

Brother: What do you mean by Erudition?

Coach: Erudition is the quality of having or showing great knowledge or learning. You know, *"scholarship."*

Brother: What kind of scholarship?

Coach: Academic study or achievement; learning of a high level or grade.

Brother: Okay. This is all starting to make sense now.

Coach: Excellent!

Brother: But you also used the words *"Wisdom"* and *"Resources"* a moment ago.

Coach: Yes I did. Beauty is impossible to bring forth without Wisdom to Contrive and Resources with which to Build.

Brother: Resource... don't you mean *"Strength?"*

Coach: I said, *"Resource"* because the true meaning of *"Strength"* is *"Resource"* and it is for this reason that Hiram, King of Tyre, was chosen; he had the resources!

Brother: But what does any of this have to do with saying The Master's Word?

Coach: But we're not talking about something you utter here.

Brother: We're not?

Coach: We are not.

Brother: Then about what are we talking?

Coach: The Word that was lost. It cannot be conveyed in this manner.

Brother: It can't?

Coach: Yes. It can't.

Brother: Why not?

Coach: Let's go through it.

Brother: Okay.

Coach: The Master's Word is something you *are*, and you aren't *it* unless you do the Work to develop, in a masterfully manner, all aspects of Wisdom, Strength and Beauty to Perfection.

Brother: To Flawlessness?

Coach: No. Not to flawlessness; to maturity. You know, *"suitability"* and not *"flawlessness."*

Brother: Oh!

Coach: And this must be done so that all three are present and in agreement with each other.

Brother: Like, they must harmonize with each other?

Coach: Yes! Harmony is but one of many aspects of this *"agreement"* between the three, but it best describes what must be present.

Brother: Is this why, within the Allegory, Grand Master Hiram was unable to give the Ruffians what they demanded?

Coach: Yes. They were each lacking all three aspects and agreement as represented by the three Grand Masters and hence the ruffians themselves did not embody what The Word represented – Mastery.

Brother: Mastery?

Coach: Yes. They died never knowing that the reason for their not getting The Word was their lack of Skill Development in three distinct domains - they lacked Strength, Wisdom and Beauty and the necessary agreement that must exist among them to manifest Mastery.

Brother: Why isn't this understood by more?

Coach: That's a great question. Part of grasping what was Lost is realizing that the story conveying this understanding is an allegory and, hence, all characters represent something else.

Brother: And members think it's literal?

Coach: Yes. This is why so many Brothers misunderstand the allegory. They have yet to climb the last seven of fifteen steps to cultivate the mastery required to understand allegories.

Brother: To understand that the story is not historical?

Coach: Yes! It is an allegory. It is not an historical account. There is no King Solomon. There is no King Hiram. There is no Hiram Abiff. These names are used for characters representing other things and are only used to deliver an underlying message.

Brother: Agreed!

Coach: The message is clear though, at least to those who understand allegory.

Brother: What's the message?

Coach: When you develop yourself so that you have Wisdom, Beauty & Strength present in what you do and all are in agreement, you are the incarnation of The Master's Word.

Brother: And when you don't?

Coach: When you don't do this, you're not.

Brother: And the ruffians?

Coach: The ruffians refused to do this. They thought it was something they could *"get"* from someone else.

Brother: Why not?

Coach: It was their focus; they could never obtain The Master's Word because they were seeking something outside themselves rather than seeking those specific things needing to be cultivated within.

Brother: They refused to do the necessary Work as though they could simply get it from another.

Coach: Yes! This is also the exact reason you should always be suspicious of anyone or any system that says that they have the Lost Master's Word and that you can get it from them if you simply pay some more money and go through yet another ceremony. The claims simply do not Pass the Acid Test.

Brother: I can see that.

Coach: So, let's go back to the original question. What I'm saying is this. Cunning Craftsmanship was lost. This occurs every time a man dies who invested a lifetime in developing and cultivating masterful skills. All that he could do, as a result of what he developed, dies with him. When such a person dies, The Master's Word is lost.

Brother: That's a tremendous loss!

Coach: Yes.

24. Substituting the Substitute

You are to have no other gods as a substitute for me. – Exodus 20:3, Deut 5:7

A Brother Asks: If you were offered an opportunity to substitute any word for the word currently given to candidates at the end of the third degree, what word would you use to provide a more significant experience of their raising?

Coach: That is one of the best ritual related questions I have ever been asked.

Brother: Thanks. But you're not answering it yet. Would you?

Coach: Yes. Of course I would. And thanks for asking.

Brother: You're welcome.

Coach: I would use a word that communicated very warmly and personally a firm *"hello and welcome"* to candidates.

Brother: Like a simple *"hello?"*

Coach: Yes and no.

Brother: Please explain.

Coach: Yes, it should be simply stated, like *"hello"* or *"welcome."* No, it should communicate so much more than just *"hello and welcome."*

Brother: What would you want it to communicate beyond the simple *"hello and welcome?"*

Coach: Besides communicating the, *"hello; welcome"*, I would use a word that also communicated acknowledgement and reception that is offered only to intimate family members.

Brother: So the word would be understood to be conveyed only to intimate family members?

Coach: Yes.

Brother: What else?

Coach: It should also confirm, through its use, a strong foundation of understanding between the conveyer and the recipients.

Brother: Such as?

Coach: A variety of well-understood upfront personal agreements.

Brother: For instance?

Coach: It would communicate that no harm will come to the recipients by way of the person saying it.

Brother: What else?

Coach: It would communicate that a place has been opened up in the life and heart of the person conveying it for the persons hearing it.

Brother: What more can you offer??

Coach: It would communicate a clear understanding that God is reciprocated love and, as such, there is also an obligation upon all parties that this will be the foundation of what is shared and practiced between them.

Brother: All these crucial sentiments would be communicated by saying just this one word?

Coach: Yes. Furthermore, each would be understood by all who heard and knew this word.

Brother: Is it possible that a word exists that communicates all these vital sentiments?

Coach: Yes. Not only is it possible, it actually does exist.

Brother: It does?

Coach: Yes. It does.

Brother: Where does it exist?

Coach: Currently this word is spoken in lands where Arabic is the indigenous language. Additionally, there are many associated languages that use variations of this word to communicate these and similar sentiments.

Brother: That would mean this word has a root language from which it originated.

Coach: Yes, it would. That root language is Aramaic.[24]

Brother: I understand that Aramaic has been around for quite some time.

Coach: Yes. It's been around for about thirty-one hundred years and it was a language of commerce.

Brother: Thirty-one hundred years? That would mean it would likely to have been used during Solomon's time.

Coach: Agreed! It is very likely!

Brother: And you said it is used in commerce?

Coach: Yes.

Brother: Like when a king of that period discussed business with another king trying to purchase lumber or hire workers?

Coach: Yes. I see that you are making some important connections.

Brother: I am. And if such a king were to see the other king for the first time in a long time, he would greet him with this word?

Coach: Yes. He would.

Brother: And if someone were to welcome a new Brother into a society, letting him know that he was part of a family now, secure in the knowledge that he would be treated as such, he would be greeted with this word?

Coach: He would.

Brother: Brother! Please tell me. What is this Arabic word?

Coach: That word is *"Marhabon"*, although it does have a variety of other spellings.[25]

Brother: *Marhabon?*

Coach: Yes. *Marhabon.*

Brother: How is this word pronounced?

Coach: It's not so obvious to those who do not speak the native tongue.

Brother: Are you saying it cannot be properly pronounced just by trying to sound it out phonetically?

Coach: You might hazard[26] a guess and try.

Brother: I'd rather you walk me through it. Would you?

Coach: Yes. The *"r"* and, sometimes the *"n"*, appear to be near silent. This gives the word either a *"ma hah' bah"* or a *"ma' hah bah"* phonetic pronunciation, depending upon the region and dialect.

Brother: That's not how I might try to pronounce it.

Coach: With my not speaking Arabic, I would only be able to take my best guess and hope who was hearing it would understand what I'm trying to communicate or rely upon speakers of the language to inform me as to how to pronounce it.

Brother: This is a very interesting word. I can see why you would want to use it as the first word spoken to candidates once they become full members of the Fraternity.

Coach: I'm glad you see what I am trying to convey my Brother.

Brother: *Ma hah' bah* my Brother!

Coach: *Ma' hah bah* my Brother!

Brother: Yes, I see the value of having this word as the first word spoken to those who are newly raised members. It should be communicated thereafter as well. Why is it not?

Coach: It is not used because we have a substitute. And until future generations discover and begin to use the real word, a substitute for the real thing is all that we shall have.

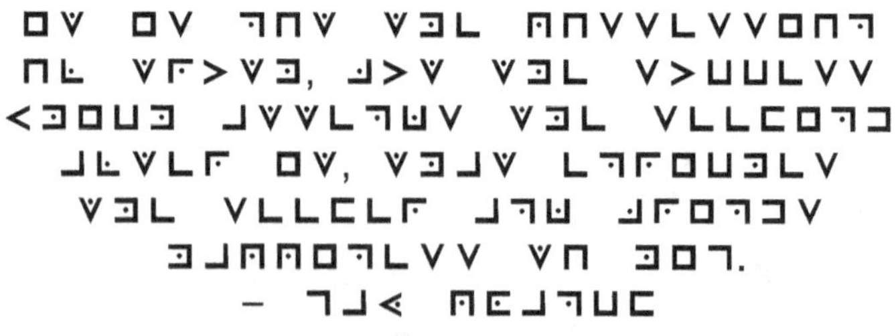

Endnotes

---

1 a.k.a. *"Morality Play"*

2 Guilds are similar to today's trade unions.

3 **Ruffians** – The traitors of the Third Degree are called *Assassins* in Continental Freemasonry and in the advanced Degrees. The English and American Freemasons have adopted in their instructions the more homely appellation of *Ruffians*. The fabricators of the high Degrees adopted a variety of names for these Assassins, but the original names are preserved in the instructions of the York and American Rites.

There is no question that has so much perplexed Masonic antiquaries as the true derivation and meaning of these three names. In their present form, they are confessedly uncouth and without apparent signification.

Yet it is certain that we can trace them in that form to the earliest appearance of the legend of the Third Degree, and it is equally certain that at the time of their adoption some meaning must have been attached to them. Brother Mackey was convinced that this must have been a very simple one, and one that would have been easily comprehended by the whole of the Craft, who were in the constant use of them.

Attempts, it is true, have been made to find the root of these three names in some recondite reference to the Hebrew names of God. But there is in Doctor Mackey's opinion, no valid authority for any such derivation. In the first place, the character and conduct of the supposed possessors of these names preclude the idea of any congruity and appropriateness between them and any of the divine names.

And again, the literary condition of the Craft at the time of the invention of the names equally precludes the probability that any names would have been fabricated of a recondite signification, and which could not have been readily understood and appreciated by the ordinary class of Freemasons who were to use them.

The names must naturally have been of a construction that would convey a familiar idea would be suitable to the incidents in which they were to be employed, and would be congruous with the character of the individuals upon whom they were to be bestowed.

Now all these requisites meet in a word which was entirely familiar to the Craft at the time when these names were probably invented. The *Ghiblim* are spoken of by Anderson, meaning *Ghiblim*, as stonecutters or Masons; and the early amounts show us very clearly that the Fraternity in that day considered *Giblim* as the name of a Mason; not only of a Mason generally, but especially of that class of Masons who, as Drummond says, "put the finishing hand to King Solomon's Temple"—that is to say the Fellow Crafts. Anderson also places the *Ghiblim* among the Fellow Crafts; and so, very naturally, the early Freemasons, not imbued with any amount of Hebrew learning, and not making a distinction between the singular and phıral forms of that language, soon got to calling a Fellow Craft a *Giblim*.

The steps of corruption between *Giblim* and *Jubelum* were not very gradual; nor can anyone doubt that such corruptions of spelling and pronunciation were common among these illiterate Freemasons, when he reads the Old Manuscripts, and finds such verbal distortions as *Nembroch* for *Nimrod*, *Euglet* for *Euclid*, and *Aymon* for *Hiram*. Thus, the first corruption was from *Giblim* to *Gibalim*, which brought the word to three syllables, making it thus nearer to its eventual change.

Then we find in the early works another transformation into *Chibbelum*. The French Freemasons also took the work of corruption in hand, and from *Giblim* they manufactured *Jiblime* and *Jibulum* and *Jabulum*. Some of these French corruptions came back to English Freemasonry about the time of the fabrication of the advanced degrees, and even the French words were distorted. Thus in the Leland Manuscript, the English Freemasons made out of *Pytagore*, the French for *Pythagoras*, the unknown name *Peter Gower*, which is said so much to have puzzled John Locke.

So we may through these mingled English and French corruptions trace the genealogy of the word Jubelum; thus, Ghiblim, Giblim, Gibalim, Chibbelum, Jiblime, Jibelum, Jabelum, rind, finally, Jubelum. It meant simply a Fellow Craft, and was appropriately given as a common name to a particular Fellow Graft who vas distinguished for his treachery. In other words, he was designated, not by a special and distinctive name, but by the title of his condition and rank at the Temple.

He was *the Fellow Craft*, who was at the head of a conspiracy. As for the names of the other two Ruffians, they were readily constructed out of that of the greatest one by a simple change of the termination of the word from *um* to *a* in one, and from *um* to *o* in the other, thus preserving, by a similarity of names, the idea of their relationship, for the old works said that they were Brothers who had come together out of Tyre. This derivation to Doctor Mackey seems to be easy, natural, and comprehensible. The change from *Giblim*, or rather from *Gibalim* to *Jubelum*, is one that is far less extraordinary than that which one half of the Masonic words have undergone in their transformation from their original to their present form. ; Encyclopedia of Freemasonry; Albert Mackey (as previously provided.)

4 **Morality** – Short for *"Morality Play."*

5 **Why Ethiopia?** by Earl D. Harris, P.G.M., Georgia Member, S. California Research Lodge; https://tseday.wordpress.com/tag/hiramic-legend/

6 **Ethiopia** – A tract of country to the south of Egypt, and watered by the upper Nile. The reference to Ethiopia, familiar to Freemasons, as a place of attempted escape for certain criminals, is not to be found in the English or French accounts, and Brother Mackey was inclined to think that this addition to the Hiramic legend is an American interpolation. The selection of Ethiopia, by the old authorities, as a place of

refuge, seems to be rather inappropriate when we consider what must have been the character of that country in the age of Solomon. Encyclopedia of Freemasonry; A. Mackey

7 **fare** (n) – Old English *fær* "journey, road, passage, expedition," from strong neuter of *faran* "to journey" (see fare (v.)); merged with *faru* "journey, expedition, companions, baggage," strong fem. of *faran*. Original sense is obsolete, except in compounds (wayfarer, sea-faring, etc.) Meaning "food provided" is c. 1200 (Old English also had the word in the sense "means of subsistence"); that of "conveyance" appears in Scottish early 15c. and led to sense of "payment for passage" (1510s). Meaning "person conveyed in a vehicle" is from 1560s.

fare (v.) - Old English *faran* "to journey, set forth, go, travel, wander, make one's way," also "be, happen, exist; be in a particular condition," from Proto-Germanic **faran* "to go" (source also of Old Saxon, Old High German, Gothic *faran*, Old Norse and Old Frisian *fara*, Dutch *varen*, German *fahren*), from PIE **por-* "going, passage," from root **per-* (2) "to lead, pass over." Related: fared; faring.

8 Some USA Rituals have the conversation between the searchers and either the ship's captain or a seafaring man, instead the wayfaring man.

9 Fellow craft numbers vary with some rituals having fifteen fellow crafts which do not include the three assassins within their ranks.

[10] **Ruffian** – One who ruffs; one who does not follow suit; one who skips over what is usually necessary and required to accomplish a desired end.

[11] Based upon the Extensive Lists, Instructions and Works found within: *Building Ruffish - Uncommon Field Guide for Uncommon Masonic Education - Volume 6*

[12] **Cleft** (n) – a fissure, rift, break or split; a deep division between two parts of the body.

[13] Brothers who remain complacent with their unsquared Work and untempered Cement.

[14] **Ruffians, Names of the** – Theosophical and occultist writers have argued that the combined endings of the three names of the Ruffians form together the mystical, Brahmin AUM; and from this they argue that Freemasonry conceals mysteries from the Far East, etc. Historians have found that Speculative Freemasonry arose in England and developed out of Operative Freemasonry which was for some four or five centuries spread over Britain and Europe; an argument composed of speculations about so slight a fact as the endings of three names is not sufficient to overthrow the massive accumulation of data collected by those historians.

Equally disastrous to the theory is the fact that at one time or another, the Ruffians have had other names, and have differed in number; also, the *a, o, m* endings became crystallized in the Ritual after the founding of Speculative Freemasonry. In the old catechism called *The Whole Institutions of Freemasons Opened*, a short document published in Dublin in 1725,

occur these curious sentences: "Your first word is Jachin and Boaz is the answer to it, and Grip at the forefinger joint.—Your 2nd word is Magboe and Boe is the answer to it, and Grip at the Wrist. Your 3rd word is Gibboram, Esimbrel is the answer."
The origin of the Ruffians themselves is undiscovered; perhaps when the Ritual came to be enacted, instead of being largely composed of a set of drawn symbols with verbal explanations, they were introduced and given their names; if so, the endings may be nothing more than a form of verbal symmetry. (The subject of the many instances of verbal symmetry in the Work, along with other forms of symmetry such as 3, 5, 7, etc., awaits research; if the research were conducted according to the canons of literary analysis, in addition to historical analysis, it might yield light on the origin of the form of the Work now in use. Symmetry cannot be either coincidental or accidental, but must imply redaction, or editorship, or authorship. Bro. and Prof. David Eugene Smith has suggested that the three names are suspiciously like certain old variations on the Hebrew word for "jubilee."; Encyclopedia of Freemasonry; Albert Mackey

[15] London: H. Serjeant, 1760 p. 53

[16] Ruffians, Names of the; ibid

[17] Jubilee, Encyclopedia of Freemasonry; A. Mackey

[18] Joual is a working class dialect of Québécois (Quebec) French

[19] Or *"lumière";* Old French *lum 'light',* from Latin *lumen.*

[20] Joual shares many features with modern *Oïl* languages, such as *Norman, Gallo, Picard, Poitevin* and *Saintongeais* though its affinities are greatest with the 17th century *koiné* of Paris. Speakers of these languages of France predominated among settlers to New France. Their usage varies.

[21] Quote from learned Brother Coleman Hill.

[22] Literally *"overseer."*

[23] As denoted by the first artificer of sharp instruments of brass and iron, Tubal-Cain, along with his two brothers and a sister, as a good example of this; this is straight from biblical text and Stonecraft lore.

[24] Syriac (Aramaic, Assyrian) is a form of Aramaic, a language whose many dialects have been in continuous use since the eleventh century BC.

[25] *"Marhaba", "merhaba", "maraba", "meraba" or "mehrabani"*, among many others!

[26] **hazard** (v) – *"put something at stake in a game of chance,"* 1520s, from Middle French hasarder *"to play at gambling, throw dice"* (15c.), from hasard. Related: Hazarded; hazarding.

www.ingramcontent.com/pod-product-compliance
Lightning Source LLC
Chambersburg PA
CBHW071847230426
43671CB00012B/2098
* 9 7 8 0 9 9 1 1 0 9 4 4 9 *